Religious Beliefs Revisited:
The Tep Heseb Editions
By: Chavis Tp-hsb Ahaw McCray

© Kofi Piesie ReSearch Team. © Same Tree Different Branch

Same Tree Different Branch Publishing
Copyright 2021 by Kofi Piesie Research Team

All right reserved. No part of this book may be reproduced or transmitted in any form or by any means, electronic or mechanical, including photocopying, recording, or by any information storage and retrieval systems without the written permission of the publisher.

Printed in the United States of America

Table of Contents

Acknowledgments

Dedicated Foreword

Foreword - Raheem Otunji-Jabar Williams

Introduction

Chapter 1 - Life and times of C. McCray

Chapter 2 - Enter the Fake "Woke" & Surpassing feel good rhetoric straight to No Pseudo

Chapter 3 - Rape of the Collective African Mind

Chapter 4 - The Science of Belief

Chapter 5 – Biblical Historicity??

Chapter 6 – The Abrahamic Concept of God, Hermeneutics, Cognitive Psychology and My Assessment

Chapter 7 - My 2 cents on The Are Africans Atheist Conversation

Acknowledgments

In this journey, we call life my wife, who birthed my children, has been with me through my extreme highs and extreme lows and deserves the first acknowledgment. Though my love for knowledge and reading worked her nerves many days, I know the manifestation of my ideas to physical form excites her just as much as me. I appreciate her for being the first person to advise me to think about writing something with all these new things I was learning. Our situation motivated me to wanna make something out of nothing and show her none of this educating myself stuff was a waste of time. If anyone has had to put up with my growth and changes in perspective, it's her. There were times where things got rough due to my unsubscribing to Christianity. Yet, on 7/24, we will have been married 6 years and together 10+ yrs. I thank you for being the Ryder I always knew you were and having my babies who motivated me to be something better than what I was.

I thank my momma and Aunt Lisa for the strongest encouragement and best support a person could have. I always wanted to make the both of you proud of my intellect, and now I'm getting that chance to take that opportunity. I thank my brothers Chad and Chase for the love and support and momma used to tell us we all we got.

I want to acknowledge my granny, the greatest woman walking this planet in my eyes. There is no one more dependable or caring than Verda Belle. Only Big mama Ella Johnson comes close. These women are the wisest I know and deserve recognition. I acknowledge my father for making me read them Encyclopedia volumes, memorize bible books, making me do current events, and being my biggest critic. Thank you for the inspiration through false ideas you had of me not liking to read. I want to thank my aunt Val who always knew I was intelligent and capable of things beyond my imagination. I thank my Grandfather Leroy for making sure I took care of my mama and Granny. He also always told me how smart I was all my life and that I had a special purpose in life. I want to acknowledge my Papa James "Duke" McCray, who showed me what a father and a man of integrity was along with my father and helped mold the foundation to create the man I am today. I appreciate your death revealing to me exactly what a legacy was and putting fire under my butt to start leaving a legacy of my own. I acknowledge all the McCrays, Hawkins, Thealls, Slaughter, Perkins, and long live Marlon Gomez while I'm at it free JD, Lil Robert, BG, and Binky.

I thank big brother Kofi Piesie for giving me an opportunity and being an example I can learn from to utilize on my own later. I acknowledge Shawn for keeping my steel sharper than a ginsu blade. I appreciate Sutekh for your role in me jumping down with KPRT. I appreciate the leveling up in the stock game from Setepenre and the wisdom of Tchalla. All of y'all gave me a lane to do something productive with my life and a legacy in adding me to the team, and I am forever grateful. I appreciate Harold Johnson for being a behind-the-scenes big homie giving me books and Ankh West and Wudjau Iry Maat for being ambassadors of scientific literacy. They're examples of great teachers that I soaked up game from to build my warrior scholar reasoning and intellectual arsenal. Shout to my fb friends NuNu and Juju y'all Kno who y'all are. Shout out Mike Rainey, Big Cliff, Felipe (Flop Po) Mav Monk, Raheem, Chris, and Seth Hunter; the whole Scarborough 2005 varsity basketball team, and shout out to Robert Rann. Shout out to my supervisor Danny, co-worker Donny boy, Braden Marshall, Jus Bates, my little cousins Darrel and Darrien, and all they sisters. Shout out to the lil homie Marquez Boyd, Deneshia Banire A SICKLE CELL WARRIOR FOREVER. MY DAY 1 HOMIE SINCE I BEEN IN HOUSTON.

I will always love you and make myself available for whatever you need from the kid, Jasmine Smith who still support me to this day no matter how much time pass much love go your way, can't forget my Damu BROTHER FROM ANOTHER MOTHER NELSON "Neno" HUGHES, Tee, Shawon "Redd" Minex Ms. Mickey and my other south side family, Michelle, Drew, Bradley, Mirthy, Terrance Chris, Uncle Danny and anybody else that seen me come up from nothing and showed love. I hope this work is edifying and cherished as I put my all into it.

Dedicated Foreword

Dear husband,

I am extremely honored to witness all your hard work and dedication towards accomplishing your goal of becoming an author. All of the reading, researching, falling asleep listening to videos, and debating on Facebook 12 hours a day (lol) paid off. What simply amazes me is how you've grown to retain so much knowledge. Knowledge that can help our people understand the importance of knowing the truth who they are and where they come from. I am proud to be your wife.

Shaibrittany McDowell-McCray aka "Sweetness" aka Honey Buns aka Love of your Life

Foreword

"To a man that I've literally seen grow online in mind and responsibility. When I first noticed you in debate groups, you were sharp, quick-witted, and you continued to excel. I came to know you as a dedicated man committed to his family as a father and a husband but even more so to the interest of his people. I am honored and proud of your accomplishments."

Raheem Otunji-Jabar Williams

Introduction

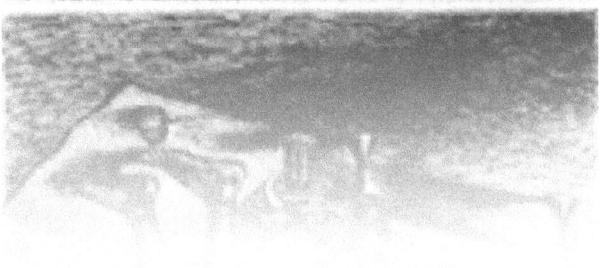

I thought I'd use the introduction to take the opportunity to explain the cover of my book and link it to the subject matter in the book as there is no direct obvious connection but rather a figurative one that the image and symbolism inspired. "Mangbetu King Munza at court in 1870, brandishing a prestige scepter and much adorned with regalia Engraving by J. D. Cooper. Reproduced in George Schweinfurth, Artes africanae: Abbildungen und beschreibungen von erzeugnissen des kunstfleisses centralafrikanischer völker "(Leipzig: F. A. Brockhaus, 1874). This is the description given below the caption of the image. Above the image reads, "Grasping power.

This scepter belonged to a Mangbetu king. Its sickle-shaped blade (also suggestive of a throwing knife) shows how a lethal weapon could become an extension of a king's grasp, communicating his power. The handles of such prestige objects were often enhanced with wrapped copper, pewter, or iron wire. Among Mangbetu, copper was deemed even more precious than iron, and the use of this softer metal underscored a blade's symbolic rather than violent purpose. (Blades of Power and Prestige, 2021 https://africa.si.edu/exhibitions/current-exhibitions/striking-iron-the-art-of-african-blacksmiths/blades-of-power-and-prestige/)

While this publication isn't specifically about the Mangbetu, a Central Sudanic ethnic group in the Democratic Republic of the Congo, living in the northeastern province of Haut-UeleI. I am utilizing the symbolism of this particular knife and substituting it with this book as it will be a lethal weapon to falsehoods and poorly constructed logic dealing with historical realities of religious belief in regards to the Abrahamic religion and black people across the diaspora. It will give you the power to see outside of the little box that is your area of awareness. It should equip your comprehension in regards to religious belief to see things with clarity that are outside your circumference of awareness. This is power that enables you to obtain understanding through knowledge and wisdom of historical objective truth. The grasping power of this figurative prestigious blade of power in book form will assist in slicing through the chains of willful or innocent ignorance and psychological chains of conceptual framework slavery. It will offer you tools to challenge common beliefs and traditions engrained via sociological conditioning, which is the "sociological process of training individuals in a society to act or respond in a manner generally approved by the society in general and peer groups within society. The concept is stronger than that of socialization, which refers to the process of inheriting norms, customs, and ideologies." (Social conditioning, 2020 retrieved from https://archive.unescwa.org/social-conditioning).

"Democratic Republic of the Congo; Mangbetu artist

Pipe bowl

Wood

H. 14 cm (5 1/2")

University of Iowa Stanley Museum of Art, The Stanley Collection of African Art, X1986.486

"When the explorer George Schweinfurth visited the Mangbetu in 1874 he noted that the people were passionate smokers. He saw King Munza smoking a six-foot pipe in" a very formal manner, assisted by a courtier whose only duty was to hold the pipe when the king was not inhaling. These pipes, and all of the court paraphernalia Schweinfurth saw, were non-figurative. Indeed, no figurative sculpture was reported among the Mangbetu until well after the era of early explorers in the late nineteenth century (Keunnen 1984).

Like the female figure in the Stanley Collection (X1986.530), this beautiful little pipe bowl bears the marks of female beauty valued by the Mangbetu, including the elongated skull produced by binding the head in infancy with raffia bands. The length of the head is accentuated by the elaborate, flaring hairstyle, supported on thin, stiff, raffia strips that are inserted in the hairstyle as it is plaited. She bears long, dark lines that were painted on the face before important public appearances.

-Professor Christopher D. Roy, 1991

Featured in Everyday Endeavor

MEDIUM

wood

TAGS

pipe

COLLECTION

Stanley Collection of African Art MUSEUM

(University of Iowa Stanley Museum of Art Retrieved from https://africa.uima.uiowa.edu/media/photos/show/2823?back=chapters%2Feverydayendeavor%2Fsmoking-and-drinking%3Fstart%3D9)

Given the fact the Mangbetu have been mentioned, it would only be right to explore their Religious Beliefs through their system, which we now refer to as kimoyo. The Mangbetu creator god is known as Kilima or Noro. Ara is a god associated with water and was known to take the form of an animal that was to be feared. They also believed that human souls could be reborn as animals. The Mangbetu royalty demanded that their ancestors be venerated. Likundu (bad spirits) demanded offerings by punishing those who ignored them with sickness and misfortune. These spirits could be directed at an individual by witches. The job of the diviner among the Mangbetu often involved uncovering and correcting the work of witches (Mangbetu, n.d retrieved from https://africa.uima.uiowa.edu/peoples/show Mangbetu#:~:text=The%20Mangbetu%20creator%20god%20is,that%20their%20ancestors%20be%20venerated)

The first thing that should be addressed is the idea that witches are conceptually foreign, as is the term "witch," which is in reality a term retrofitted into the paradigm of the African via contact with those who spoke old English. "Witch (n.) Old English wicce "female magician, sorceress," in later use especially "a woman supposed to have dealings with the devil or evil spirits and to be able by their cooperation to perform supernatural acts," fem. Of Qld English wicca "sorcerer, wizard, man who practices witchcraft or magic," from verb wiccian "to practice witchcraft" (compare Low German wikken, wicken "to use witchcraft," wikker, wicker "soothsayer").(Etymonline, 2001)

We can be almost certain that this concept was one that was utilized to articulate the authors western interpretation of Mangbetu ritualistic psychology, therefore to utilize it to explain any type of role or position in this African society would be problematic and only offering a surface understanding of the individuals responsibilities who is being categorized as a witch. While there may have been women whose role was to be in charge of ritual practices, we clearly find men across the continent who holds similar roles and responsibilities. When dealing with African culture, we must learn to understand that the English language presents problematic issues of agency in the meaning behind their indigenous concepts. Most of what we read on these cultures is in English sometimes interpreted directly from foreigners who are detached from a proper worldview necessary to grasp these societal mores and norms of a particular people. "term "trans-substantive" refers to doctrine that, in form and manner of application, does not vary from one substantive context to the next." (Marcus. D,2014) Therefore a Tran substantive error would be the fallacy of attempting in form and manner of application to apply one substantive context to another, which should not be done if the goal is to obtain an accurate interpretation of the subject matter in question.

The most accurate way to determine what the term used to represent their concept of God one would need to have full command over their language. Without a proper grasp on the lexical structure and meaning, one is simply surface scraping concepts that have layers and layers of deeper meaning. A full linguistic treatment is necessary to obtain these deeper meanings; without such, it wouldn't offer proper Justice in explanation. Further analysis outside of the current focus of this particular publication is necessary to provide answers to gain a greater understanding of Mangbetu concept of God.

	tp hsb	correct method, norm, etiquette, metre (of speech) [noun] D1 - Z1 - J2 - Y1
	ꜥḥꜣ	fight, battle [noun] D34
	ꜥḥꜣ	Warrior [noun - title] D34
	ꜥḥꜣ	fight [verb] D34 - A24
	ꜥḥꜣw	war, (weapons of) war [noun]
	ꜥḥꜣw	arrows, weapons [noun] D34 - G1 - G43 - T11B
	ꜥḥꜣw	warrior [noun - title] D34 - G1 - G43 - X1 - Z4 - A24

Another phrase that may have captured the reader's attention on the cover that many aren't familiar with is "tep heseb edition." You may have visited my Facebook profile and seen /tp hsb ahaw/ and had no clue what that meant or what it was. I have heard everything from people thinking I changed my name to people assuming it's an acronym that they just don't know what the letters represent for a gang or click. The reality is I translate exactly what it means under my picture: /tp hsb/ (Correct method) /ahaw/ (Warrior). It isn't a name given to me by any group or organization. It is honestly a title I created and chose to embody influenced by innovative ancient AFRIKAN genius to always be a reminder that the idea of white man science is fallacious.

It was the ancient /rmtch/ (Egyptians) along with the other Nile and Niger valley civilizations who demonstrated high scientific understanding and methodology thousands of years before some the most influential individuals in Greek thought even put 2 and 2 together. As I will go into later, scientific literacy and methodology have been the biggest game-changers in my intellectual journey. They have been monumental tools in navigating the world of information we currently reside in. Social media has created echo chambers of people who have poor methodology due to a myriad of reasons ranging from lack of competence to willful ignorance and everything in between. A common particular mindset that plagues the African American sector of social media is attributing scientific thought to the white man in a fallacious attempt to characterize, demonize, and minimize, and overgeneralize science as a whole as the white man invention but will ironically in the next sentence tell you about how the ancient Egyptians were black and the 1st to do everything. One saying I try to live by is

"When you know better, you do better" This is something I champion and always challenge those around me.

Willful ignorance is not okay. If we know high scientific thought existed in /km.t/ (Egypt aka place name see toponym), we have to act like it and understand before there was the scientific method, there was /tp heseb/. I was introduced to this term by the Seshew Maa Ny Mdw Ntr group who have various publications, a YouTube channel, a Facebook group, and a class that teaches how to transliterate and translate the script to help revive the language. On their website, they offer us a better understanding when they elaborate excellently, "As it relates to African traditions…. The transmission of these explanations of occurrences/facts (which are theories by scientific use of the term) was done by way of what is called today the various "figurative speech." The "figurative expressions" and the realities behind those figurative expressions were usually transmitted together in Initiatory Environments. This is exactly what historical societies did and continue to do. What many call "religious" texts are expositions of the scientific theories related to the body of people to whom those texts belong.

The above claim shows a lack of understanding of what a scientific theory is and its application as well as what myths are and how they are compiled. The word "myth" as it applies to African traditions are a set of narratives that make use of what we call today "figurative speech." These narratives are indeed, explanations of facts or occurrences. The "scientific method" as practiced in the various scientific fields of study is expressed in ancient Nile Valley literature. Indeed, indigenous peoples did, in fact, examine and devote time to cultivate information and gather it into narratives to teach peers and future generations.

In km.t 'Kemet' we have an example (one of many) of the scientific method being used and declared:

tp-Hsb n hAt m xt rx ntt nbt. That is how this sentence is scientifically transliterated, but it expressing the meaning in English as "The correct method of investigating nature to know all that exists." There are several texts where we will see this phrase tp-Hsb being used in the context of what we would call today "The Scientific Method."

tp-Hsb n hAt m xt rx ntt nbt
"The correct method of investigating nature to know all that exists."

In the above sentence, the phrase tp-Hsb means "correct method, best method," as the above translation shows. The word tp of itself is used as «best, preferred,» and Hsb is used as «an account, a reckoning, computation». When used together and in context, this phrase means «correct method, accurate method, rules of». The people of kmt 'Kemet' used a set of methods to arrive at rx 'rekh' «knowledge». These methods are expressed in various texts and generally correspond to the methods now described as "the scientific method." tp-Hsb is a key factor in research as it employs a set of rules necessary for understanding things in all its aspects and phenomena. The above sentence can be broken down to give a better detail as:

tp-Hsb – correct method

n – genitive: of

hAt m – to descend into, used in context as "to investigate, dig deep into an issue, question, problem, to study, to comprehend by moving into."

xt – things

rx – to know, knowledge

ntt nbt – all that exists

The logical flow of the set of rules tp-Hsb generally corresponds to the procedural flow in what is called the "scientific method" today. They are:

tp – "beginning" – this is the first step in the process called tp hence "beginning." At this step, the precise enunciation of the problem to be solved, with elucidatory examples, is given.

mi Dd n.k – "if one says to you that." This is the stage of definition, where everything is made clear and distinct, and all the relevant terms are explicitly and precisely defined. The expression mi Dd means "according to that which is said," that is, the process of reasoning is to be addressed to a precisely formulated problem.

ptr – "What?" In Ranykemet grammar ptr 'peter' stands at the beginning of questions with the function of eliciting a logical predicate. A question is an expression of inquiry that invites a reply or solution. At this stage, then, the student is directly required to ponder and analyze ptr the problem under examination.

irt mi xpr – "correct procedure." This is the stage of demonstration, that is, the mental process of showing something to be true by reasoning and computation from initial data. The process of calculating is based on a careful set of mathematical formulas.

rxt.f pw – "solution, it is known." This is knowledge rxt 'rekhet' found, and grasped in the mind with clarity or certainty. The solution is regarded as true beyond doubt. The student has shown the requisite know-how, that is, the knowledge and skill required to do something correctly. The solution is evident, thanks to the demonstration by a dependable logical procedure.

sSmt – "examination of the proof." This is the review of the whole body of evidence or premises and rules that determine the validity of a solution. Such an examination of a logical proof always leads to a further conceptual generalization. Thus, the ancient people of Kemet had the technique of forming concepts inductively.

gm.k nfr – "you have found good." This is the concluding stage. To be able to do something, and find it correctly done, means that it was done as it should be done. gmi «to find» is to obtain by intellectual effort, and bring oneself to a mental awareness of what is correct, precise, perfect nfr. To arrive at a logical conclusion and find that the conclusion withstands critical scrutiny is an achievement in the art of deduction. The adverb nfr «well» implies that the solution is convincing so that a contradiction is impossible. The concluding observations are mainly confirmatory. Nevertheless, the rigor of the entire process is evident in the method, and the result is objectively known in all truth." ("The Scientific Method in Kemet - Sesh Medew Netcher - The Ancient Egyptian Hieroglyphic Writing System" https://seshmedewnetcher.com/the-scientific-method-in-kemet/)

Asar Imhotep's Aaluja Cyena Ntu Religion & Philosophy vol. 2 adds to our understanding on page 225 where he demonstrates the importance of method in km.t providing evidence via the lexicon of the ancient Egyptians "care and concern for methodology seen through several terms related to method. For example: /tp/

(way (of doing something) method, cipher, key example. /t p-hsb/ (the correct method; norm, reckoning. /md.w/ method. /md.t/ (matter, affair)

/tp n jrt/ (working method, method" (Imhotep, 2020) He goes on to cite the same sentence the Seshew broke down citing the Rhind Mathematical papyrus as the primary he draws the conclusion "Thus, the rmt we're not simply concerned with mere surface speculations about reality, or with myths to explain phenomena, but with the right course of action in the necessary steps to know for sure " mysteries and all things secret" concerning nature (/ht/). The phrase tp- hsb "correct method" can be broken down into tp "way" or model (the best example for a logical process and hsb "to take into account" the word for method means to

31

take into account the correct procedure or the right path this implies that there are other options that were considered hypothesis but given the evidence this is the best course of action (i.e the best way/road to the truth). (Imhotep, 2020)

I see myself as a correct method Warrior and intend these tep heseb edition(s) I plan to work on in the future and the one you are currently reading to be a reflection of that. Hopefully, this opportunity given to me to explain has offered edification.

Chapter 1
Life and times of C. McCray

Many people who have known me for longer then the past 10 years have witnessed an intellectual maturity in the area of spirituality and religion that I believe has pushed some people away. I am not of the opinion that this distancing from some is the result of being personally offended or having a personal grudge. I think that some people are willingly ignorant of historical realities. Others only need religion to cope as a mechanism for them to deal with life. That information and knowledge that I came into create cognitive dissonance and distortions for many.

As I continue further in this chapter, I will define these terms like cognitive dissonance and cognitive distortion in an effort to offer edification as to where I am coming from with this analysis. I want to emphasize that these are not insults but strictly observations from a psychological perspective. But before I get into the assessment, I would like to offer personal insight as far as my past, and how I came to the conclusions, I have drawn.

I didn't always question religion, the Bible, or God. For a long time, I considered myself a god-fearing Christian who just wanted to go to heaven and be like Jesus. My early memories of church are at Bella Vista Baptist Church in Studewood, a historic neighborhood in Houston's north (or Nawfside as we like to say down here in the 3rd coast), Where my Pawpaw was Deacon. It was the place where both sides of my family could be found on any given Sunday of a year. My parents were married there, and I was baptized there (2×)

It's where we learned to pray and where we studied the Bible via Sunday School and Sunday sermons. I learned about the characters in The Bible and learned to memorize the Bible's books, different verses of the Bible. We developed our morals around the Bible. We were disciplined based on the Bible. The Bible was where we drew from to obtain wisdom and understanding, and it was held in the highest regard. In our minds, it embodied the title of HOLY and was the tool with all the answers and guided us whether we were at Bella Vista or in San Diego at the San Diego Church of Christ (non-denominational) or a Baptist

Church in San Diego or a Houston Church of Christ.

Bible and its God were the common denominators at any location. Especially since my dad was in the navy, and we went where he went, which was San Diego, a completely different environment than Houston. San Diego is extremely diverse compared to Houston especially depending on which areas you are in, but even in areas of poverty, there are a multitude of ethnicities in the city all over. This being the case joining a non-denominational church that's multi-ethnic, you get an experience a little different from your Southern Baptist Church. The first thing you recognize is singing and the music but also a difference in the way the Bible is interpreted essentially or more the delivery of sermons.

Here, at this particular church in San Diego, not much zealous homily was expressed, and there was more a focus offering insightful positive life messages in a what would Jesus do modern NIV bible reading sentiment versus old school Southern Baptist KJV reading paradigm.

Both churches were essentially positive places for the members, and the churches helped them deal with this thing we call life. My purpose and intent here is not to bad-mouth these establishments as they were foundational in my development in my adolescence.

However, I will objectively expose the reader to the realities of the psychology, historicity, and literary devices behind many of the ideas and concepts influenced by the book we call the Holy Bible and its contents. We also will objectively examine sociological dynamics associated with religious belief.

To be completely honest, as a kid though going to church was a positive thing, it was not where I personally wanted to spend my Sunday morning and afternoon. I, like others, basically was forced to continue to attend church all through my adolescence and teens. As a preteen, I started to question concepts in the Bible like who gets to go to heaven and who doesn't and why certain things were okay in the book, but other things weren't.

I used to ask my mom were the native tribes, monks, Hindu people around the world who didn't know Jesus were they going to hell, and she would tell me that basically everyone will get a chance to know Jesus, and if they don't accept him, then they would perish basically.

As a kid, I thought that was pretty messed up. An older Aunt who is now deceased by the name of Valerie used to question a lot of these ideas associated with the church in the Bible as well. At the church of Christ, there is a paradigm of once you are a certain age and start dating, you stay inside the church as far as where you are to look for your mate.

My father and a lot of people look at the church as something of a cult. He preferred Baptist and was loyal to his church in Houston, bringing his family Bible from when he was married to San Diego, which was the King James version. He used to make me memorize the books over and over and over until I could recite them all. When I wasn't doing that, I was in some type of workbook that my mom or the church gave me to study different parts of the Bible.

My mom always gave me scriptures to read and had me go in the back of the book and look up different lessons by searching keywords and finding scriptures that fit. You can spend a lot of my time doing that because there are so many scriptures and different contexts using these words, but the habit makes you pretty creative at extracting wisdom from random pieces of literature.

The older I got, the more I chose to try and utilize the book on my own to deal with life and cope with everyday struggles. One thing I struggled with dealing with the Bible was separating what was literal and what was figurative. Certain parts of the Bible, like parables of Jesus, were philosophical and could be interpreted in a lot of ways in a positive manner. But they were also parts that, if taken literally I found disturbing and just automatically assume that they were not literal.

CHAPTER 2

Enter the Fake "Woke" & Surpassing feel good rhetoric straight to No Pseudo

These logical conundrums were at the root of what pushed me away eventually from subscribing to that particular ideology viewing it in hindsight. It took me almost 27 years before I started critically examining things I thought I knew. My journey wasn't a snap your fingers immediate transition; it was gradual. It's what Nipsey Hussle deemed a Marathon. For a long time, I avoided confrontational discussions regarding religious ideologies because I was taught not to question the Bible or God and not to lean on my own understanding through religious texts. For those who know me now know, I get a kick out of it. I think part of the reason why I avoided confrontation of discussions on the topic is also because I wasn't really studied.

All I read was the Bible from time but not much else. The most I'd argue a person down was that God made marijuana and they said it in the scripture he was cool with it. The first real passionate discussion I had in regards to the subject of Christianity was 2011 maybe with my dad when he was in school taking philosophy. He was challenging my beliefs basically not intentionally but explaining to me what was going on in the classroom. I could not argue logically; I made countless appeals to emotion and incredulity. Maybe a year later, my roommate Desean came home one day awakened by some Hebrew Israelite knowledge and hit me with the question, when did the letter J originate. Cuh stumped me because I had no clue. He started hitting me with the Jesus ain't real spill. All I could do to defend my belief was rationalize that the character in the story and tattoo on my forearm was a pretty good guy and never did anything wrong to anybody so real or fake he was cool with me because I didn't know for sure whether the guy was even real, I was indoctrinated. These were My first sign, and I had literally no clue. Sometime later, I watched a Kevin Wesley video that asked a question as to what nationality Jesus would have been and that basically he was a Jew, and I had never thought about that. That one question blew my mind because as a Christian, we are taught to do what Jesus does, and for the first time in my life, I had to ask myself, okay, why are we Christians if he comes from a family of Jewish people. No one I got my Bible information from could answer that question preachers and all.

After getting that paradigm-altering question from Kevin Wesley, I subscribed to his channel, and I ended up hearing him mention Ray Hagins, who I eventually ended up following information-wise every day and learning about Maat and Kemet and contradictions and flaws in scripture. That was my beginning of becoming "woke" from there, I decided to reprogram my mind and deal with knowledge over belief. I didn't know if saying in Jesus name at the end of a prayer worked, so I stopped praying. I didn't want to believe anything from that point. I ended up getting invited to a Hebrew Israelite vs Kemetic group and started soaking game quietly, gathering resources through the group's members like Raheem and Marquez. I could tell they knew what they were talking about. That group led me to Sa Neter channel, watching Polight debates. I resonated most with Amen Ra Squad scholarly method source up or shut up approach. All this was to build a foundation on objectivity, so my readers will know I came from thinking just like you. The only bias I have is against ignorance and tomfoolery. So, at this point, this is where I transition to how I got here in this book you're reading, demonstrating the scholarly characteristics and reason why KPRT made me a part of the team.

In previous volumes, you were educated on terms like religion, African traditional religion/systems, and a historical documentation of European and Arab views of superiority over Africans. Going forward, the terms and concepts I introduce should add to that which you already have. I'll begin this quote from a book called The Rape of the Mind.

CHAPTER 3

Rape of the Collective African Mind

"The knowledge that the human mind can be influenced, tamed, and broken down into servility is far older than the modern dictatorial concept of enforced indoctrination....
Throughout history, men have had an intuitive understanding that the mind can be manipulated, and elaborate strategies have been worked out to achieve this end.

The continual intrusion into our minds of the hammering noises of arguments and propaganda can lead to two kinds of reactions. It may lead to apathy and indifference, the I-don't-care reaction, or to a more intensified desire to study and to understand."(Meerloo,1956)

"What we deem a religious education is characterized as religious indoctrination. Indoctrination is the process of inculcating a person with ideas, attitudes, cognitive strategies or professional methodologies " (Snook, 1972)

A quick google search will inform you that it is "The process of teaching a person or group to accept a set of beliefs uncritically." (Oxford, n.d)

Detaching myself emotionally from my journey knowledge-wise, that definition articulates exactly what took place. It isn't me trying to down any religion, simply the objective reality. I literally took everything in that book at face value. The very first few verses in the book demonstrate we as a collective people did uncritically accept this. The person supposedly writing Genesis was nowhere to be found if we are to take it seriously.

To break this down quickly so far, we have a religious text and a religious ideology introduced to the majority of African-American people during slavery. "A dictionary defines sociology as the systematic study of society and social interaction.

The word "sociology" is derived from the Latin word socius (companion) and the Greek word logos (speech or reason), which together mean "reasoned speech about companionship" (Little, n.d). The approach social scientists take they understand that religion exists as an organized and integrated set of beliefs, behaviors, and norms centered on basic social needs and values.

Given the bible was essentially a foreign religious text to the African has one ever pondered just exactly whose needs and values fuel these integrated beliefs, behavior, and norm?

People who are religious come from societies. Societies have culture. In that culture is where you'll find religious beliefs for people. In sociology, there are two terms non-material culture and material culture. (Little, n.d) Material culture would qualify as the Bible non-material would be the belief in Christianity.

One way to honestly explain the state of many black people who have uncritically accepted this material culture of as an authority of any is via the term Deculturalization.

"Deculturalization is the process by which an ethnic group is forced to abandon its language, culture, and customs. It is the destruction of the culture of a dominant group and its replacement by the culture of the dominating group" (Branch, 2014). Deculturalization is a slow process due to its extensive goal of fully replacing the subordinate ethnic group's culture and language, and customs. Methods of deculturalization include:

Geographical segregation

Forbidding education to the dominated group

Forceful replacing of language

Superior culture's curriculum in schools

Instructors are from the dominant group

Avoiding the dominated group's culture in curriculum

Books like The Religious Instruction of the Negro offer primary source material. The author shows the blueprint in the table of contents.

"HISTORICAL SKETCH OF THE RELIGIOUS INSTRUCTION OF THE NEGROES FROM THEIR 1ST INTRODUCTION INTO THE COUNTRY IN 1620 To THE YEAR 1842 DIVIDED INTO 3 PERIODS

The First Period — From their introduction in 1620 to the first census in 1790: a period of 170 years.

1. Account of the Introduction Of NEGROES into the Colonies under the Government of Great Britain.

2. Estimated Negro Population of the Colonies at the Declaration of Independence and census of 1790.

3. Efforts for their Religious Instruction, both Great Britain and America, year by year, during this period,

The Second Period From the first census in 1790 to 1820: a period of 30 years, year by year.

The Third Period —From 1820 to 1842: a period of 22 years, year by year

1. Efforts year by year. Manual of instruction,

2. Action of Ecclesiastical Bodies, and of different Denomination of Christians,

3. This period — a period of revival as to this particular duty, throughout the Southern States,

4. General Observations, in conclusion of Historical Sketch". (Jones, 1842)

This publication alone is historical documentation and support for evidence of methodically systemic deculturalization imposed on the African. They don't teach you this at school, and you sure won't have a sermon about this on Sunday morning with your favorite preacher at the church you've been going to all your life. What I learned on this Marathon is people don't even know. They may have an idea, but many people have no clue about the actual evidence that exists to demonstrate the undeniable menticide and deculturization of the African. Your local preacher probably never read How to Make a Negro Christian, so I'm almost positive he wouldn't even know how to obtain the Religious Instruction of the Negro. Even if he did, he, like any other human being who subscribes to an ideology with such passion and emotion would only rationalize and justify the persistence of the subscription.

Expanding further, the impact of Christianity on the African can be recognized immediately. "President Jacob Zuma has been cited as saying: "Christianity – introduced by European missionaries mainly in the nineteenth century – Just destroyed the safety net for orphans, elderly people and the poor" (Smith, 2011). He has also been cited, speaking at the launch of road safety and crime awareness campaign in the KwaZulu-Natal province, as saying: "As Africans, long before the arrival of religion and [the] gospel, we had our own ways of doing things. Those were times that the religious people refer to as dark days, but we know that during those times, there were no orphan[age]s or old-age homes. Christianity has brought along these things" (Smith 2011) Matsobane J Manal of the Department of Philosophy, Practical and Systematic Theology. University of South Africa, Pretoria, South Africa article states, "Optimism about the success of the missionary endeavors emerged from the 1910 Edinburgh World Missionary Conference report, which affirmed, "the possibility of completing the evangelization of the non-Christian world within a generation" (Barret 1970:39). In the same vein, many Christian scholars have predicted that by the twentieth century, Christianity's centre of gravity shall shift southwards. Christianity has indeed spread like wildfires in sub-Saharan Africa in the corresponding period in spite of the pessimism that followed as a result of the threat of rapid Islam advances (Barret 1970:39)." So not only were Africans under psychological and cultural cold calculated assault by Christianity but already defending themselves from adherents of Islam. So, when we are assessing the impact of Christianity on African people, also keep in mind the damage had already been done via Islam objectively.

To add more emphasis to the subtle indoctrination of the African, we are informed: "Christianity, as a book religion and as an institution concerned with moral life of the black people has made a significant contribution in the genesis and continued development of formal western education in sub-Saharan Africa." (Manala, 2013)

This implies the African needed Christianity as a moral compass which is fallacious and simply not true. It's a notion influenced by social norms and logic of religious zealots who view their culture and ways as superior and advanced compared to African, who is frequently characterized as a Savage, uncivilized, primitive, heathen, and other derogatory terms created to verbally disrespect the African and make them want to disassociate themselves from who they are culturally by shaming them essentially with these historically documented and normalize false labels.

To be historically fair, missionaries in Africa had moments of trying to reform treatment of The African as some were against the cruelty and horrors of slavery. "According to Sarfati (2007:122), Newton said to Wilberforce: "It is hoped and believed that the Lord has raised you up for the good of His church and for the good of the nation." Wilberforce was totally against the horrors of slavery and every cruelty, to the extent that he was even called the "Conscience of Parliament".

The task of fighting against or opposing the slave trade was indeed the work of those filled with the Holy Spirit. Newton himself, a former slave trader, came to see (after his conversion to Christ) "that since the slaves were also created in the image of God, the slave trade was wrong in itself and could not be humanized. He left the trade, became friend with the great evangelists George Whitfield (1714-1770) and John Wesley (1703-1791) and his brother Charles (1707-1788), became a minister and testified to King George III (1738-1820) about the atrocities of the slave trade" (Sarfati 2007:122). The commitment of Christian men and women to root out slavery was akin to Christ's commitment and resolve to save the world. Regarding Malawi, Mkandawire (2009:63) states that, by the time Dr. Law left Livingstonia in 1927 after 52 years of missionary service, several evil social practices had been abolished in Malawi "for instance, slave trading had been stopped, and the trial by poison ordeal was no longer practiced."

In short, the gospel message brought about real transformation, a transformation that instilled divine principles and humaneness in the socio-political lives of African people." (Manala, 2013)

While I can acknowledge these acts of humanity, the facts still remain in the process of this change of heart and sentiment towards slavery; it didn't include respecting the culture of these people; they were converting to Christianity realistically.

At the same time, historically and objectively, it can't be omitted that there have been plenty of our ancestors who utilize Christian values to rally others to combat oppression and injustice. Examples of these individuals specifically include MLK, Nat Turner, Rosa Parks, Marcus Garvey, and Harriet Tubman. South Africa has instances where we find that "African nationalism in South Africa emerged as a force to be reckoned with during the 1950s, and was inspired by the influence of certain Christian missionary institutions (e.g., Lovedale and Fort Hare University, institutions at which many black people received higher education). Indeed, in the 1950s, the Christian church and missionary institutions of higher learning served as a catalyst for heightened political awareness among Africans, African nationalism, and the African realization that there was a need for true liberation. This was the time of the Defiance Campaign, launched in 1952; the Campaign made its mark on 26 June of the same year in Port Elizabeth, when the harbors, the city, and everything came to a total halt. The Campaign culminated in the Sharpeville massacre of 1960 (Walshe 1991:27).

Walshe (1991:27) makes an important statement about the nature of the socio-political struggle in South Africa: "The struggle against discrimination in South Africa, as many have argued, is theological as well as political. This is so, in the words of Ben Marais, because 'Apartheid erodes the very basis of humanity." Christianity and its values, as well as the active participation by church ministers and church members, provided the liberation struggle with an enormous "boost". The church literally became, in the words of Walshe (1991:28), "a site of the struggle".

Walshe (1991:28) notes that prophetic Christianity was thus "able to interact, and even too mesh, with the liberation struggle". By the mid-1980s, then, prophetic Christians were playing a significant role in exposing the illegitimacy of the South African government and in empowering the liberation movement. (Manala, 2013)

One extremely interesting quote from Manala article comes from a section dealing with the impact of Christianity in regards to African health is a belief of superior efficacy in church-related medical services. "Church-based facilities were known to be humane and "people-friendly", which obviously made them popular. Indeed, according to Good (1991:2): "African populations everywhere almost invariably seem to believe that health workers employed in the church-related health services provide care that is superior to their Ministry of Health counterparts because they are trained to understand the connection between body and soul and show greater compassion for human suffering." (Manala, 2013)

While contextually, that may have been a positive in the moment of the circumstances being faced but from the perspective of solely science, that type of believe can be dangerous and lead to bad decisions made based on lack of scientific literacy being applied while attempting to use unsound fallacious reasoning to gauge the metrics of proper scientific medical training in dealing with health versus relying on alleged connections to bodies and souls.

While to some of the Christian faith I may sound unnecessarily critical, my earlier position of not letting Christianity off the hook because of those positive things that occurred that it had something to do with is echoed here in the article to further substantiate the point I was making stating " Although Christianity, couched as it was in western civilization, brought some relief to Africa in freeing it from some of its woes (albeit, in some cases, only partially - e.g. Africa's belief in witchcraft), there are certain areas in which the religion did serious harm to the African way of life.

Notwithstanding missionaries claims that they were concerned to protect indigenous peoples and their interests, the fact remains that some missionaries at least sought to advance the interests and culture of their colonial masters. Mtuze (2003:2) rightly asserts: "The study shows very clearly that the missionaries, consciously or unconsciously, had a double agenda in that they were also de facto agents of the colonial powers who subjugated the propagation of the Word to cultural and political imperialism." For this reason, much of Africa's ways of life were frowned upon, if not totally demonized. Pityana (1999:137) attests to this: "Christianity declared some African practices pagan, and the church was a pervasive influence on family practices." This led to a serious identity crisis for many Africans, a crisis that resulted in African self-hatred and self-denigration. The nineteenth century was therefore noted for the emergence and gradual increase of conflict between the two cultures (Mtuze 2003:8).

In later years, black Africans managed to salvage, at massive cost (including death), their self-respect, self-love, and pride in their blackness, largely thanks to the Black Consciousness Movement in South Africa and elsewhere in Africa. Partially as a result of this, Africans in South Africa consciously chose and used African, rather than Christian, names (Pityana 1999:138)." (Manala, 2013)

"Christianity led to the demise of the African customs, which it viewed as pagan and evil; the religion also led to the implementation of apartheid (to which it gave its theological support), and undermined the leadership role of women."(Manala, 2013)

In an article titled "Christian Imperialism and Trans Atlantic slave trade" the ultimate reality is articulated to perfection in the first paragraph when it states "The transatlantic trade in Africans was founded on Christianity. Religion was key in motivating Prince Henry of Portugal, later called Henry, "the Navigator" (1394–1460), to put in motion Europe's aggressive and ruthless expeditions to Africa. Henry was not only the governor of Algrave Province, who managed a large economic infrastructure based on the unbridled grasp of enormous wealth from trans-Saharan commerce, but he was also the administrator of the Order of Christ, the Portuguese successor to the Knights Templar, a famous Western military order founded in the aftermath of the First Crusade at Clermont on November 27, 1095.

As one of the best fighting units, the Soldiers of Christ prompted a series of striking maritime exploits, ensuring the safety of Europeans who made pilgrimages to Jerusalem. It is important to note that during this historical period, the feudal states of European countries were just beginning to unite and major religious wars were being fought between Christians and Muslims, especially the Moors in Morocco. Henry trained men to sail from Portugal, down the west coast of Africa in search of the limits to the Muslim world, in order to halt the Islamization of West Africa and to accelerate the spread of Christianity. In order to further God's intentions for humankind, Ogbu Kalu contends that within the context of religious logic, papal bulls offered rights of patronage to Henry, authorizing him to appoint clerical orders for evangelization and to fend off competing European interests. According to

Peter Russell, Henry the Navigator considered conversion and enslavement as interchangeable terms, experiencing no cognitive dissonance in using Christianity as a civilizing agent for making converts into slaves" (Cannon, K. G. (2008). Christian Imperialism and the Transatlantic Slave Trade. Journal of Feminist Studies in Religion, 24(1), 127–134. http://www.jstor.org/stable/20487919)

CHAPTER 4

The Science of Belief

In the Indian Journal of Psychiatry, an article titled The Biochemistry of Belief informs us, "Beliefs are basically the guiding principles in life that provide direction and meaning in life. Beliefs are the preset, organized filters to our perceptions of the world (external and internal). Beliefs are like 'Internal commands' to the brain as to how to represent what is happening when we congruently believe something to be true. In the absence of beliefs or inability to tap into them, people feel disempowered.

Beliefs originate from what we hear – and keep on hearing from others, ever since we were children (and even before that!). The sources of beliefs include environment, events, knowledge, past experiences, visualization etc. One of the biggest misconceptions people often harbor is that belief is a static, intellectual concept. Nothing can be farther from the truth! Beliefs are a choice. We have the power to choose our beliefs. Our beliefs become our reality…Research findings have repeatedly pointed out that the emotional brain is no longer confined to the classical locales of the hippocampus, amygdala, and hypothalamus.

The sensory inputs we receive from the environment undergo a filtering process as they travel across one or more synapses, ultimately reaching the area of higher processing, like the frontal lobes. There, the sensory information enters our conscious awareness. What portion of this sensory information enters is determined by our beliefs. Fortunately for us, receptors on the cell membranes are flexible, which can alter in sensitivity and conformation. In other words, even when we feel stuck 'emotionally', there is always a biochemical potential for change and possible growth. When we choose to change our thoughts (bursts of neurochemicals!), we become open and receptive to other pieces of sensory information hitherto blocked by our beliefs! When we change our thinking, we change our beliefs. When we change our beliefs, we change our behavior." (Indian J Psychiatry. 2009 Oct-Dec; 51(4): 239–241)

The church you go to, the religious literature you read, and all the concepts and experiences you had/have attached are the sensory inputs we receive externally to process internally.

How critically we examine this external information is relative to how much other information we previously processed that deals with reason and logic. It's also relative to how much we uncritically processed and accepted of these sensory inputs. Scientific literacy offers an approach to falsifying uncritically processed data by challenging the mind to be rigorously critical of flaws and errors in logic in regards to the data being processed.

Certain ways of reasoning/thinking create difficulty in comprehension of nuanced concepts involved in the critical analysis that is scientific literacy. Religious reasoning would fall into the categorization of problematic thinking/reasoning in a particular context. To support the reality of this type of reasoning exist in a 2009 article indicates "Our analysis reveals 3 psychological dimensions of religious belief (God's perceived level of involvement, God's perceived emotion, and doctrinal/experiential religious knowledge), which functional MRI localizes within networks processing Theory of Mind regarding intent and emotion, abstract semantics, and imagery. Our results are unique in demonstrating that specific components of religious belief are mediated by well-known brain networks and support contemporary psychological theories that ground religious belief within evolutionary adaptive cognitive functions." (Kapogiannis. D, Barbey. A, Su. M, Zamboni. G, Krueger. F, Grafman. J, 2009)

So, the ability to project religious ideas on reality seems to be an evolutionary neurological adaption. We see evidence of some of the world's oldest symbolic artifacts in Africa interesting associated with shellfish. A paper titled "Shell fishing and Human Evolution" informs us that "Consistently large gastropods size, in the oldest known middens, suggest that human population growth cannot explain the occasional presence of symbolic artifacts or the innovative burst that coincides with the spread of fully modern Africans to Eurasia 60-50 ka… Many species exploit intertidal shell fish, but only humans regularly transport them to variably distant open air localities or rock shelters where repeated discard produces substantial shell heaps or middens.

Open-air middens dating from the Present Interglacial [Marine Isotope Stage (MIS) 1], after the 12 - 11 ka (thousands of years ago), dot lower and mid- latitude cost every where. Older open- air middens are largely unknown, probably because most that formed during previous interglacials have failed to survive exposure to the elements, while those that formed during glacial intervals are manly submerged on continental shelves. Near coastal caves and rock shelters in Southern Africa (Jacob's et al., 2008; Jerardino,2016; Klan, 2009; Kyriacou et al., 2015; Langejans etc al., 2012; Marean, 2014; Will et al., 2015) and in northwestern Africa(Campmas et al., 2015; Dibble et al., 2012; Steele, 2012; Steele and Alvearez - Fernández, 2011; Stoetzel et al.,2014) preserve middens that document central place shell fishing during the last interglacial (MIS 5), between roughly 128 and 71 ka." (Klein. R, 2019). Another excerpt tells "we therefore focus here on the postulated link between shellfish and human cognition. In the final section, we also address the human evolutionary implications of gastropod size the African Middle Stone Age (MSA) middens dated between 126- 60ka.

Some MSA middens contain what are widely regarded as the world's oldest symbolic artifacts more compelling and abundant examples of African Later Stone Age (LSA) and coevals of European Upper Paleolithic after 50ka" (Klein. R, 2019)

An article titled the Science of Religious Belief elaborates further, stating: "Why have humans, throughout history and across cultures, shown a strong tendency to believe in the existence of superhuman intentional agents and attached this belief to notions of morality, misfortune, and the creation of the world? The answer emerging from the cognitive science of religion appears to be that explicit beliefs are informed and constrained by the natural and cross-culturally recurrent operation of implicit cognitive systems. Successful god concepts resonate with the expectations of these implicit systems but also have attention-demanding and inferentially-rich properties that allow their integration into various areas of human concern.

Theological concepts may deviate from these natural cognitive moorings but require special cultural scaffolding, such as Whitehouse's two Modes of Religiosity, to do so and constitute additions to, rather than replacements of the religious beliefs supported by implicit cognitive systems." (Barret. J, Lankan. J, 2008)

Study.com compares implicit vs explicit attitudes via an internet article titled "Implicit vs. Explicit Attitudes: Definition, Examples & Pros/Cons". Before I quote the difference, I think it's first important to explain that quick change in terms in regards to belief and attitude to demonstrate to the reader the connection between the two. "Attitudes arise out of core values and beliefs we hold internally. Beliefs are assumptions and convictions we hold to be true based on past experiences. Values are worthy ideas based on things, concepts, and people…. Attitudes are not the same as behaviors." (Kumar. M, 2018) So to reiterate what was quoted attitudes develop out of belief.

"Explicit attitudes are attitudes that are at the conscious level, are deliberately formed, and are easy to self-report. On the other hand, implicit attitudes are attitudes that are at the unconscious level, are involuntarily formed and are typically unknown to us." ((Implicit vs. Explicit Attitudes: Definition, Examples & Pros/Cons)

This should add clarity to the answer given to the question posed in the science of Religious Beliefs when we see the use of terms implicit cognitive system and explicit beliefs. We should understand that we are talking about conscious thoughts when we speak on explicit beliefs, and we are speaking on unconscious systems that operate around us in society when we speak on cognitive implicit systems. It is necessary to put these things into context to fully grasp what is being read.

One argument used by believers to validate their beliefs is the fact that the concept of biblical God is all over the world, so it must be True if everyone knows about him. An article in Nature journal helps explain this phenomenon.

"Most humans believe in a god, but many do not. Differences in belief have profound societal impacts. Anthropological accounts implicate bottom-up perceptual processes in shaping religious belief, suggesting that individual differences in these processes may help explain variation in belief. Here, in findings replicated across socio-religiously disparate samples studied in the U.S. and Afghanistan, implicit learning of patterns/order within visuospatial sequences (IL-pat) in a strongly bottom-up paradigm predict 1) stronger belief in an intervening/ordering god and 2) increased strength-of-belief from childhood to adulthood, controlling for explicit learning and parental belief. Consistent with research implicating IL-pat as a basis of intuition and intuition as a basis of belief, mediation models support a hypothesized effect pathway whereby IL-pat leads to intuitions of order which, in turn, lead to belief in ordering gods. The universality and variability of human IL-pat may thus contribute to the global presence and variability of religious belief." (Weinberger, A.B., Gallagher, N.M., Warren, Z.J. et al., 2020)

In the conclusion of the article, the findings are as follows "The present findings support a conceptually aligned hypothesis that individuals who more readily learn, at an implicit level, patterns that are actually present in the environment may be biased toward belief in ordering Gods. Conversely, those who less readily learn available patterns via IL-pat may be less predisposed toward such beliefs." (Weinberger, A.B., Gallagher, N.M., Warren, Z.J. et al., 2020)

This, for me, speaks volumes in explaining the variability in belief across the globe in regards to God. This very informative chapter enlightens the reader on scientific function and mechanism of belief in general in our lives but offers in-depth resources and information to tap into the particulars. I hope this information offers the reader edification in regards to the subject of belief.

Chapter 5

Biblical Historicity??

Charges of historicism are frequently critical, implying that the subject is historically inaccurate or ignorant (for example, an ahistorical attitude). It can also describe a person's failure to frame an argument or issue in a historical context or to disregard historical fact or implication. (Pepper, 1993) Biblical narratives are constantly challenged from everything from the characters to who wrote the text, when they wrote it, what language it's written in. If you are Christian or Hebrew or Catholic or any subtype of an Abrahamic religion, have you asked yourself these questions? Have you done the work to support your belief and turned it into something that you now know based on actual evidence? Or have you relied on faith and never challenged "God's word"? Well, today's your lucky day. I took the time to compile everything I could find scholars that deal with the historicity of the Bible from my journey with sources attached.

"In the following decades, Hermann Gunkel drew attention to the mythic aspects of the Pentateuch, and Albrecht Alt, Martin Noth, and the tradition history school argued that although its core traditions had genuinely ancient roots, the narratives were fictional framing devices and were not intended as history in the modern sense. Though doubts have been cast on the historiographic reconstructions of this school (particularly the notion of oral traditions as a primary ancient source), much of its critique of biblical historicity found wide acceptance. Gunkel's position is that if we consider figures like Abraham, Isaac, and Jacob to be actual persons with no original mythic foundations, that does not mean that they are historical figures. ...For even if, as may well be assumed, there was once a man-call "Abraham," everyone who knows the history of legends is sure that the legend is in no position at the distance of so many centuries to preserve a picture of the personal holiness of Abraham. The "religion of Abraham" is, in reality, the religion of the legend narrators which they attribute to Abraham."[1]. (Gunkel 1997, p. lxviii)

"In the United States, the biblical archaeology movement, under the influence of Albright, counterattacked, arguing that the broad outline within the framing narratives was also true so that while scholars could not realistically expect to prove or disprove individual episodes from the life of Abraham and the other patriarchs, these were real individuals who could be placed in a context proven from the archaeological record. But as more discoveries were made and anticipated finds failed to materialize, it became apparent that archaeology did not, in fact, support the claims made by Albright and his followers. Today, only a minority of scholars continue to work within this framework, mainly for reasons of religious conviction" (Mazar, Amihay Archaeology of the land of the Bible, 10,000-586 BCE. Garden City, NY: Doubleday. ISBN 978-0385425902. 1992)

BIBLICAL HISTORY AND ISRAEL'S PAST

Changing Views of Scholars in Their Own Words The dramatic shifts in the study of the patriarchs and matriarchs that occurred during and after the 1970s can be illustrated by quotations from two works on the history of Israel separated by several decades. In a history initially written in the 1950s, John Bright asserted, "Abraham, Isaac, and Jacob were clan chiefs who lived in the second millennium B.C.... The Bible's narrative accurately reflects the times to which it refers. But to what it tells of the lives of the patriarchs, we can add nothing."1 Assessing the situation in scholarship four decades later, William Dever, in 2001, concluded, "After a century of exhaustive investigation, all respectable archaeologists have given up hope of recovering any context that would make Abraham, Isaac, or Jacob credible 'historical figures.'"2 1. John Bright, A History of Israel, 4th ed. (Louisville: Westminster John Knox, 2000), p. 93. 2. William G. Dever, What Did the Biblical Writers Know, and When Did They Know It? What Archaeology Can Tell Us About the Reality of Ancient Israel (Grand Rapids: Eerdmans, 2001), p. 98.

"... historical figures but as literary creations of this later period. Though the evidentiary underpinnings of this thesis were new, the thesis itself was quite similar to the views held by Alt and Noth. Thompson, Van Seters, and others had shown that the earlier scholarly consensus of a second-millennium date for the traditions depended upon coincidences and harmonization of evidence that could not be sustained. Thompson provided one of the most representative statements of this change in the study of Israel's past: "[N]ot only has 'archaeology' not proven a single event of the patriarchal traditions to be historical, it has not shown any of the traditions to be likely. Based on what we know of the Palestinian history of the Second Millennium B.C., and of what we understand about the formation of the literary traditions of Genesis, it must be concluded that any such historicity as is commonly spoken of in both scholarly and popular works about the patriarchs of Genesis is hardly possible and totally improbable" (Megan Bishop Moore; Brad E. Kelle (2011). Biblical History and Israel S Past: The Changing Study of the Bible and History. Wm. B. Eerdmans Publishing. P. 62. ISBN 978-0-8028-6260-0.)

William Dever stated in 1993 that "[Albright's] central theses have all been overturned, partly by further advances in Biblical criticism, but mostly by the continuing archaeological research of younger Americans and Israelis to whom he himself gave encouragement and momentum. ...The irony is that, in the long run, it will have been the newer "secular" archaeology that contributed the most to Biblical studies, not "Biblical archaeology" (Dever, William (March 1993). "What Remains of the House that Albright Built?". The Biblical Archaeologist. 56 (1): 25–35. Doi:10.2307/3210358. JSTOR 3210358.)

Many scholars believe that the "Deuteronomistic History" preserved ancient texts and oral tradition elements, including geo-political and socio-economic realities and specific information about historical figures and events. However, large portions of it are legendary, and it contains many anachronisms. (Mazar, Amihai (2010). "Archaeology and the Biblical Narrative: The Case of the United Monarchy" (PDF). In Kratz, Reinhard G.; Spieckermann, Hermann; Corzilius, Björn; Pilger, Tanja (eds.). One God – one cult – one nation archaeological and biblical perspectives

(Submitted manuscript). Berlin; New York: Walter de Gruyter. Pp. 29–58. Doi:10.(Israel Finkelstein; Neil Asher Silberman (2001). The Bible Unearthed: Archaeology's New Vision of Ancient Israel and the Origin of Sacred Texts. Simon and Schuster. Pp. 81–82. ISBN 978-074322338 (Israel Finkelstein; Neil Asher Silberman (2001). The Bible Unearthed: Archaeology's New Vision of Ancient Israel and the Origin of Sacred Texts. Simon and Schuster. Pp. 81–82. ISBN 978-0743223386.) Garstang originally announced that he had found fallen walls dating to the time of the biblical Battle of Jericho, but later revised the destruction to a much earlier period. (Holland, Thomas A. (1997). "Jericho." In Eric M. Meyers (ed.). The Oxford Encyclopedia of Archaeology in the Near East. Oxford University Press. Pp. 220–224) Kathleen Kenyon dated the destruction of the walled city to the middle of the 16th century (c. 1550 BCE), too early to match the usual dating of the Exodus to Pharaoh Ramses, based on her excavations in the early 1950s. (Kenyon, Kathleen M. (1957). Digging up Jericho: The Results of the Jericho Excavations, 1952–1956. New York: Praeger. P. 229.)

The same conclusion, based on an analysis of all the excavation findings, was reached by Piotr Bienkowski.[43] (Bienkowski, Piotr (1986). Jericho in the Late Bronze Age. Warminster. Pp. 120–125.) By the 1960s, it had become clear that the archaeological record did not support the account of the conquest given in Joshua: the cities which the Bible records as having been destroyed by the Israelites were either uninhabited at the time or, if killed, were damaged at widely different times, not in one brief period. According to Israel Finkelstein, the consensus for the conquest narrative was abandoned in the late 20th century.[40](Israel Finkelstein; Neil Asher Silberman (2001). The Bible Unearthed: Archaeology's New Vision of Ancient Israel and the Origin of Sacred Texts. Simon and Schuster. Pp. 81–82. ISBN 978-0743223386.)

In his view, the Book of Joshua conflates several independent battles between disparate groups over the centuries and artificially attributes them to a single leader, Joshua. (Finkelstein & Silberman 2001) However, there are a few cases where the archaeological record does not contradict the biblical narrative. For example, stratum in Tel Hazor, found in a destruction layer from around 1200 BCE, shows signs of catastrophic fire, and cuneiform tablets found at the site refer to monarchs named Ibni Addi, where Ibni may be the etymological origin of Yavin (Jabin), the Canaanite leader referred to in the Hebrew Bible. (Peake's commentary on the Bible) Before its destruction, the city also shows signs of having been a magnificent Canaanite city, with great temples and opulent palaces (Hatzor – The Head of all those Kingdoms". Retrieved 2018-09-18) split into an upper acropolis and lower city; the town had been a major Canaanite city. Finklestein theorized that the destruction of Hazor was the result of civil strife, attacks by the Sea Peoples, and/or a result of the general collapse of civilization across the whole eastern Mediterranean in the Late Bronze Age, rather than being caused by the Israelites? The Books of Samuel are based on historical and legendary sources, primarily filling the gap in Israelite history after the events described in Deuteronomy. The battles involving the destruction of the Canaanites are not supported by archaeological records, and it is now widely believed that the Israelites themselves originated as a sub-group of

Canaanites. (Tubb 1998, pp. 13–14) (McNutt 1999, p. 47) (K. L. Noll, Canaan and Israel in Antiquity: An Introduction, A&C Black, 2001 p. 164: 'It would seem that in the eyes of Merneptah's artisans, Israel was a Canaanite group indistinguishable from all other Canaanite groups.' 'Merneptah's Israel was likely a group of Canaanites located in the Jezreel Valley.')

The Books of Samuel exhibit too many anachronisms to have been compiled in the 11th century B.C. For example, there is mention of later armor (1 Samuel 17:4–7, 38–39; 25:13), use of camels (1 Samuel 30:17), and cavalry (as distinct from chariotry) (1 Samuel 13:5, 2 Samuel 1:6), iron picks and axes (as though they were common) (2 Samuel 12:31), sophisticated siege techniques (2 Samuel 20:15). There is a gargantuan troop called up (2 Samuel 17:1), a battle with 20,000 casualties (2 Samuel 18:7), and a reference to Kushite paramilitary and servants, clearly giving evidence of a date in which Kushites were common, after the 26th Dynasty of Egypt, the period of the last quarter of the 8th century BCE(Redford, Donald B. (1992). Egypt, Canaan, and Israel in ancient times. Princeton,

NJ: Princeton University Press. P. 305. ISBN 978-0691000862)

"There is great scholarly controversy on the historicity of events recounted in the Biblical narratives prior to the Babylonian captivity in the 6th century BCE. There is split between scholars who reject the Biblical account of Ancient Israel as fundamentally ahistorical and those who accept it as a largely reliable source of history—termed biblical minimalists and biblical maximalists, respectively. The major split of biblical scholarship into two opposing schools is strongly disapproved by non-fundamentalist biblical scholars, as being an attempt by conservative Christians to portray the field as a bipolar argument, of which only one side is correct." (Spong, John Shelby (1992) Rescuing the Bible from Fundamentalism (Harper))

"Recently the difference between the Maximalist and Minimalist has reduced, and a new school started with work, The Quest for Historical Israel: Debating Archaeology and the History of Early Israel by Israel Finkelstein, Amihai Mazar, and Brian B. Schmidt. (Finkelstein, Mazar & Schmidt 2007)

This school argues that post-processual archaeology enables us to recognize the existence of a middle ground between Minimalism and Maximalism and that both these extremes need to be rejected. Archaeology offers both confirmations of parts of the biblical record and also poses challenges to the interpretations made by some. The careful examination of the evidence demonstrates that the historical accuracy of the first part of the Old Testament is greatest during the reign of Josiah. Some feel that the accuracy diminishes the further backwards one proceeds from this date. This, they claim, would confirm that a major redaction of the texts seems to have occurred at about that date (https://en.m.wikipedia.org/wiki/Historicity_of_the_Bible#CITEREFMazar1992)

"Biblical Genre and Structure the Bible is a vastly important religious text for people around the world, but what can we get out of the Bible as a historical text – or is it historically reliable at all? Many people read the Bible expecting everything in it to be historically accurate, but that was not actually the purpose of the authors.

To understand the Bible's historicity, we need to take its structure into account. Unlike most books you pick up and read, the Bible is actually an anthology composed of multiple books. There are two major sections: the Hebrew Bible (or Christian Old Testament), which recounts the story of the Israelites, and the New Testament, which tells the story of Jesus and the early Christians. Since they were written at different periods and for other purposes, we will look at each separately when considering their historicity.

We can classify most of the Bible under the genre of interpreted history. This means that not everything in it is historically accurate; instead, the authors were more concerned with conveying information (historical or not) that is important to their religious beliefs. When we think about the historicity of the Bible's texts, we must also remember that they have been translated and copied over time, with different motivations for each work.

For example, the King James Version, which many still read today, was commissioned by King James I of England to unite the opposing Protestant and Catholic groups in his dominion.

To achieve this, he made sure his translators' work met his theology rather than translating the text exactly how it appeared. Also, although the translations came from the Hebrew and Greek texts of the Bible, the translators did not have the same understanding of their languages and cultures that we do today. They were influenced by the Latin Vulgate, meaning some of the translations were not historically accurate.

The Hebrew Bible

Compilation

The Hebrew Bible is an anthology covering the history of the earliest Israelite people through their establishment of a monarchy, the division of the kingdom, and the eventual destruction and rebuilding of their homeland. Since it covers so much material, it makes sense that this was not written all at once.

The first five books of the Bible, called the Torah, were compiled around the 6th century BCE after various manuscripts telling independent but parallel narratives were combined into one story.

Some books of the Hebrew Bible were not even initially just one text, like the book of Isaiah, which is composed of three different sections

There are also many books like those in the Hebrew Bible that were not included in it because the compilers had two criteria for Hebrew Bible texts: they had to be initially written in Hebrew, and they had to be written by or attributed to someone who lived before the 4th century BCE.

Historicity

The historicity of the Hebrew Bible is debated by scholars and laypersons alike. Many of the Hebrew Bible stories, like that of the Tower of Babel, were probably fictional stories that act as etiologies, or explanations for the various phenomenon, like the reason we have multiple languages in the world.

The narrative in the Torah that talks about the Israelites' beginnings, their escape from slavery in Egypt, and their travel to the ''Promised Land'' has very little evidence in historical records. The first direct correlation we get between the Hebrew Bible and non-biblical sources is the mention of Shishak, or the Egyptian pharaoh Shoshenq I, in 1 King.

As the Israelites began interacting with other nations in the narrative – and getting conquered by them – we have more and more historical evidence of their activity. We know that some of the kings of Israel and Judah existed and were later conquered because we have mentions of this in texts outside of the Bible. However, some biblical places and groups of people that were once thought to have been fictional have been discovered in historical records over time, like the Hittites. They are an enemy throughout the Hebrew Bible. (Waters, T, n.d) "The Bible as a Historical Document" https://study.com/academy/lesson/the-bible-as-a-historical-document.html)

There is probably more evidence than that but what was presented was more than enough to convince me of a lack of historicity. Taking a step further, the Bible in itself is a conflated redaction. "Historical criticism understands the Bible, and by implication all other sacred scriptures, to be a compilation of texts constructed intentionally from previous layers of Judaism, borrowed from sources in other cultures in the region, and containing portions deliberately inserted by unknown priests and scribes for political and theological purposes over many generations. What begins mostly in the oral transmission is eventually written down in bits and pieces, though further transformations occur in the hands of generations of scribes who recopy and edit the text. These fragments are then selectively remembered and preserved based on the interests of those who follow. Eventually, it is redacted into a single authoritative sacred text. The redaction of the Bible is, thus, a kind of whisper down the lane in which real persons and events are mixed with fantastic elaborations and imaginations." (Grassie, 2012) For me, this falsifies this literal sentiment of the word of Bible God.

It demonstrates that humans write the book, and it is in their words written by their hands and not pre-written and cracked from the sky given directly by the hand of God to Mose. We won't even mention the logically flawed situation with the supposed author writing about the beginning of time and his death.

We will not discuss where the verses and chapter set up come from and who put them in there; just know that God didn't do it. I will leave those in ignorance who love its company.

We must be aware that there is a history of biblical interpretation. This implies multiple interpretations throughout a chronological period. Contrary to popular belief, the literal interpretation of the Bible is NOT the only interpretation. Philo, a Jew from Alexandria, Egypt (d. A.D. 50), provides us with historical evidence of the utilization of allegorical interpretation via his writings. (Bible and theology, n.d) hermeneutics is the theory and methodology for interpreting sacred/wisdom/religious texts. (Audi, R,1999). It involves rigorous textual, verbal, and criticism to draw meaning and put things into their proper context. "Hermeneutics is more than interpretative principles or methods used when immediate comprehension fails and include the art of understanding and communication. (Zimmermann, J, 2015) "There is traditionally a fourfold sense of biblical hermeneutics: literal, moral, allegorical (spiritual), and anagogical. (hermeneutics | Definition & Facts". Encyclopedia Britannica) Exegesis is utilized to draw out meaning from text objectively. Utilization of exegesis includes the original audience of the author, historical and cultural background of the text, and author. Other analysis includes grammar, syntax and literary genre. In biblical exegesis, the opposite of exegesis (to draw out) is eisegesis (to draw in), in the sense of an eisegetic commentator "importing" or "drawing in" their own purely subjective interpretations into the text, unsupported by the text itself. Eisegesis is often used as a derogatory term. (Wikipedia, n.d) So basically, what takes place in the church house by your pastor and everyone in Sunday School would qualify as eisegesis. This is because you are applying your subjective meaning to scripture that it's not based on the original audience and has nothing really to do with the original message by the original author, whoever that may be. It's a pretty word for making stuff up, and it's not the primary method of scholastic interpretation of religious texts.

"Epistemology is the study of the nature and scope of knowledge and justified belief. It analyzes the nature of knowledge and how it relates to similar notions such as truth, belief and justification. It also deals with the means of production of knowledge, as well as skepticism about different knowledge claims. It is essentially about issues having to do with the creation and dissemination of knowledge in particular areas of inquiry." (Epistemology, n.d) when assessing a belief, all this must be considered if we want to justify or falsify it. "Contemporary Anglophone philosophers of mind generally use the term "belief" to refer to the attitude we have, roughly, whenever we take something to be the case or regard it as true. To believe something, in this sense, needn't involve actively reflecting on it" (Belief, 2003). Based on this sentiment and connotation of the word and the mention of active reflection not being a priority, it's safe to conclude that belief is not the finish line. It is a starting point. To be optimistic about your belief is ok. However, holding an optimistic belief on something proven false or isn't justified is not.

CHAPTER 6

The Abrahamic concept of God, Hermeneutics, Cognitive Psychology and my Assessment

A good tool used to justify or falsify claims, or a belief is logic. I am of the position that, at times, for certain people, religious fundamentalism hinders people's ability to apply sound logic. "God of the gaps" is a theological perspective in which gaps in scientific knowledge are taken to be evidence or proof of God's existence. The term "gaps" was initially used by Christian theologians not to discredit theism but rather to point out the fallacy of relying on teleological arguments for God's existence" (Drummond,1904). It's logically flawed to insert a concept that honestly isn't clearly defined as a substitute explanation.

What is God? Where did the term come from? What does it mean? Is the word God used in the original text in the original language? Etymonline informs us that "God (n.)

Also God; Old English god "supreme being, deity; the Christian God; image of a god; godlike person," from Proto-Germanic *guthan (source also of Old Saxon, Old Frisian, Dutch God, Old High German got, German Gott, Old Norse guð, Gothic guþ), which is of uncertain origin; perhaps from PIE *ghut- "that which is invoked" (source also of Old Church Slavonic zovo "to call," Sanskrit Huta- "invoked," an epithet of Indra), from root *gheu€- "to call, invoke." The notion could be "divine entity summoned to a sacrifice. But some trace it to PIE *ghu-to- "poured," from root *gheu- "to pour, pour a libation" (source of Greek khein "to pour," also in the phrase khute gaia "poured earth," referring to a burial mound; see found (v.2)). "Given the Greek facts, the Germanic form may have referred in the first instance to the spirit immanent in a burial mound" [Watkins] originally a neuter noun in Germanic; the gender shifted to masculine after the coming of Christianity. Old English God probably was closer in a sense to Latin numen. A better word to translate deus might have been Proto-Germanic *ansuz, but this was used only of the highest deities in the Germanic religion and not of foreign gods, and it was never used of the Christian God. It survives in English mainly in the personal names beginning in Os-." (Etymonline, n.d)

To answer the question of was the term God used in the original text, one can simply utilize blue letter bible.org type in verse, for example, Genesis 1 looks at the word God, then look at strong reference H430, and we find אֱלֹהִים ĕlôhîym (Blue letter bible, n.d) Going down that rabbit hole, you come to find that The Canaanite pantheon of gods was known as 'ilhm. (Pardee, D, 1999) and that this term has possible Ugaritic influence. (Van der Toorn 1999). This will eventually lead you to theophoric names associated with the Bible books and JEPD theory which is a "documentary hypothesis posited that the Pentateuch is a compilation of four originally independent documents: the Jahwist (J), Elohist €, Deuteronomist (D), and Priestly (P) sources. The first of these, J, was dated to the Solomonic period (c. 950 BCE) (Viviano 1999, p. 40). E was dated somewhat later, in the 9th century BCE, and D was dated just before the reign of King Josiah in the 7th or 8th century. Finally, P was generally dated to the time of Ezra in the 5th century BCE. (Gmirkin 2006, p. 4.)

Books of the Bible like Obad-iah (Yahwist) and Ezeki-El (Elohist) start to paint a different narrative about how the book came to be than what you were told in a church sermon. Garfield Reid's publication Misconception & Misinformation by the Black Hebrew Israelites vol. 1 deals with a wide range of claims made by adherents to the faith, mainly Hebrew Israelites. A quote that offers insight on some textual criticism dealing with whether Moses authored the Pentateuch, he starts explaining that if you "only read first five most of the temperature a single individual couldn't have offered the tour. 18th and 19th-century German dollars of the authors of the Bible concluded that it was a composite text.

This inference is founded on portraits that appear in the Torah. 1. Vocabulary used in various parts varies greatly. 2. Divergent ideologies 3. The narrative's inconsistencies. 4 sections of the text are highly repetitive for no apparent purpose implying that variations of the same tail were used." (Reid, 2021) He then explains that in Gen 1:1, God is referred to as Elohim validating my early demonstration and elaborating on how "Elohim is a part of the first account of life but from Gen 2:4 onward second account distinctly gives an account in which Yahweh starts development of the earth." (Reid, 2021) A believer may find all kinds of ways to rationalize and justify this clear example of no sole authorship being responsible for these texts. Based on Objective analysis, I agree with Garfield's & 18th and 19th-century Scholarly position being a composite text.

The Term God is a mnemonic device for the religious mind, in my opinion. "Mnemonic n. any device or technique used to assist memory, usually by forging a link or association between the new information to be remembered and information previously encoded. For instance, one might remember the numbers in a password by associating them with expected birth dates, addresses, or room numbers." (Mnemonic, n.d,) For the religious mind, the association is with a concept that reminds them to be on their best behavior, obtain salvation, or receive eternal damnation. For some, it gives them a reminder of something bigger than them that's at work in their favor, while others simple psychological comfort. For everyone, reasoning varies and is relative to that individual.

Regarding eternal damnation, there was no hell initially, and that concept, like others in the Bible, comes from other cultures, in this instance, Zoroastrianism. "Some examples of tenets adopted by Judaism from Zoroastrianism include Ø a real, active force for evil (Angra Mainyu, whose attributes were assumed by the later Jewish Satan). Ø Concept of a final judgment of souls after death. Ø Concept of the afterlives in heaven or hell. Scholars believe that the Jews might have heard those teachings during the end of the Babylonian Exile under the Persian emperor Cyrus. (Zaehner, R.C., 1961) Before the period referred to as the Babylonian captivity (586-538 B.C.E.), Jewish philosophy held that Satan was an agent of God and tested man's loyalty to God. Sometime after Cyrus the Great permitted the Jews to return to Jerusalem, Satan became the personification of evil, a personality wherein evil originated. (Ashby, 2006) Concepts like heaven, hell, dying and coming back after three days, walking on water, getting eaten by a whale, and surviving are allegorical at best and not justified in the literal sense by any interpretation. One who studies the Bible should make themselves familiar with literary devices, which "refers to the typical structures used by writers in their works to convey their messages simply to the readers. When employed properly, the different literary devices help readers to appreciate, interpret and analyze a literary work" Literary Device, n.d) The Bible, which is literature by default, is full of literary devices, which is why you must be careful with how you interpret the text. I find literal interpretation or literalism diminishes what wisdom can be extracted from the Bible. Reading some of Philo's work, I find the allegorical interpretation extremely intriguing versus the literal, which I am not interested in. Another allegory associated with the Bible is Jesus being the son that walked on water which is supposed to be the literal Sun in the sky walking on water according to some (Stowe, 1907)

In conclusion, based on all the available evidence presented, my assessment of the religious beliefs of African Americans and the Africans, in general, is that an exceptionally biblically religious outlook is problematic in a specific context and should probably honestly be kept to oneself to protect that which you have faith and belief in. The concept of faith comes from fideism. Fideism "maintains that faith is independent of reason, or that reason and faith are hostile to each other, and faith is superior at arriving at particular truths (see natural theology). The word fideism comes from fides, the Latin word for faith, and means "faith-ism." (Amesbury 2005) Understand faith and fact are distinctive. Just because you have faith in something does not mean your belief is a fact.

Collectively we must challenge cognitive distortions that come integrated into religious thought. According to Positive psychology.com, "Cognitive distortions are biased perspectives we take on ourselves and the world around us. They are irrational thoughts and beliefs that we unknowingly reinforce over time. These patterns and systems of thought are often subtle–it's difficult to recognize them when they are a regular feature of your day-to-day thoughts. That is why they can be so damaging since it's hard to change what you don't recognize as something that needs to change! Cognitive distortions come in many forms" (Ackerman, n.d)

Doverspike, William F. "How cognitive distortions affect religious fundamentalists." Echoes my position of faith not being fact "Absolutistic thinking occurs when a person's beliefs, feelings, or opinions are equated with reality. The underlying belief is, "If I think it's So, then it's so." This process involves an Egocentric assumption (largely "unconscious" Or outside of awareness) that one's thoughts are. The reality, often accompanied by the claim. That others' beliefs are not reality. In other words, absolutistic thinkers equate their Certainty with absolute truth.

In contrast to faith, which involves a balance of belief and Doubt, absolutistic thinking consists of a sense of Certainty—which can give rise to absolute truth Claims. (Doverspike, 2016) While the contrasts faith to absolute in the context fideism type faith that essentially screams faith over everything makes absolute faith truth and qualifies the distortion. Instead of using fideism as an explanation, he stated, "Absolutism can also lead to theological arrogance, which involves an absolutistic certainty—essentially the opposite of faith. A related but broader concept is particularism, which refers to an exclusive attachment to one's group, religion, nation, or political party. Religious particularism refers to the belief that one's faith is the only path to experiencing, understanding, or worshiping the Transcendent —by whatever Name called. Another related concept is exceptionalism, the perception or belief that a country, society, institution, individual, or time period is "exceptional" (i.e., unusual or extraordinary).

Exceptionalism carries with it the implication that the referent is superior in some way, whether specified or not. Religious or theological Absolutism often involves both exceptionalism and particularism." (Doverspike, 2016) As we see, religious fundamentalism integrated into the religious paradigm is plagued with ego-driven errors in thinking. It is not productive in the collective advancement in any area for Africans.

Early in Garfield's text, he makes a statement that I immediately resonated with that I felt spoke to my conclusion "if your enemies control your religion in worldview, then they handle your culture and resources for survival l. Your enemy will put all generations at a default; we call this default slavery mental, cultural and social slavery.

Judaism, Christianity, and Islam have been destructive forces to African people because they change and distort their worldviews. Christianity Judaism Islam where on fragmented pieces of ancient African cultures, Middle Eastern cultures, and distorted facts; it was later used as a tool for the enslavement and destruction of the African mind. It consists of false hope and blind faith that has been widely accepted by the African and African American communities. Its later and present intent on the African culture and intellect has not been for the Deliverance of either of the two but for their bondage. In the early exploration or exploitation of Africa, the value was placed on its natural resource's texts were misinterpreted, and statues that were held and observance of the indigenous African ancestors became idols and considered evil when worship worshiped form of deities and gods by European and Muslim Invaders. In 1943 with the same colonizing mindset, the Spanish-borne Alexander VI decreed in the bull Inter Caetera that any land not inhabited by Christians was available to be "discovered" and claimed this allowed exportation by Christian rulers. It declared that the Catholic faith and the Christian religion be exalted everywhere. The Papal Bull states that the health of souls is cared for, the barbarous Nations are overthrown, slaves brought to the faith, and the salvation of Jesus Christ. Later, African generations were forbidden to practice what was said to be the pagan and heathen-like ways of their ancestors. Due to such leakage of false information from generation to generation, we Africans here in America have been cultivated to trade in the customs and traditions of the land we've been kidnapped from for the immoral habits, unreliable beliefs, and unjust laws of those which we've been imported. Because of that, we owe our disconnected worldview to the tremendous god-fearing religions of Islam, Christianity, and Judaism. If it weren't for its premeditated death of African cultural systems and worldview along with his fabricated pretenses, we wouldn't be able to turn the other cheek and probably say thanks for the 400 years of slavery, rape, slaughter, and destruction of our people and for allowing us to live so uncomfortably within the system that made it all possible" (Reid, 2021)

CHAPTER 7

My 2 cents on The Are Africans Atheist Conversation

As an African in America exposed to a foreign religion by default of acculturation using assimilation, the reaction to resonate more with the ideological antithesis of Atheism is only natural. But through my journey of assessing different schools of thought, I concluded that I could only be an atheist through a particular context. That context is through a lens of a theological worldview shaped through Abrahamic religion and surface Westernized understanding of African culture and what we at KPRT AND MOSSI WARRIOR CLAN identify as Kimoyo.

My goal in this chapter is to attempt to articulate and document my position on the conversation and offer much-needed context to hopefully enlighten those who have difficulty grasping the argument due to a lack of study in KIMOYO from an African worldview. I feel that because I have at points of my journey identified as an atheist, I can offer an unbiased perspective to hopefully attempt to bridge the gap in misunderstanding and misinterpretation that even I once had in viewing everything through a minimal lens of which poor understanding of African culture, agency and autonomy leads to disagreement and creates silly arguments and contention.

Three books that help form a solid understanding of this contextually significant argument are The Chronology of Human Evolution by Ankh West, Spears of the Mossi: A Historical Survey of the Minds of African Warrior Scholars, volume 1 by KPRT, and finally Beautiful Lessons About Kimoyo by Kofi Piesie. Now, these books and authors are by no means the authority on the subject matter in question. Still, they are knowledgeable African Warrior Scholars who did their due diligence on the topics they chose to put pen to pad & give us their informed understanding via their highly informative work and independent research. I am forever grateful for their efforts as they lead to my opportunity to connect these dots and attempt to explain the missing context that is usually omitted or minimized in the haste of passionate live dialogue.

So, from my understanding, the issues stem from the use of the term God applied to African "deities," who qualifies as an atheist, and why. I believe starting from the latter using Ankh's and then shifting focus to Spears of the Moss, I particularly Kofi's chapter 3 Confusion misunderstanding ignorance about African Traditional Religion and How it's Under Attack by Western Society and Our Own Unstudied and end with Beautiful Lessons about Kimoyo will offer answers and clarification to the topic. I will utilize quotes from Asar Imhotep's YouTube presentation I extracted via screenshot to help substantiate where I stand on the matter.

But before I do that, I'd like to take the time to clarify my angle. I identify myself in the context of westernized theological terms as a theological noncognitivist. "Theological noncognitivism is the non-theist position that religious language, particularly theological terminology such as "God," is not intelligible or meaningful, and thus sentences like "God exists" are cognitively meaningless." (Conifer, 2002) "It may be considered synonymous with ignosticism (also called theism), a term coined in 1964 by Sherwin Wine, a rabbi and a founding figure of Humanistic Judaism" (Spiegel, 1965)

The focus of theological noncognitivists laid out is meaning regarding the use of the term God. In its modern meaning in 2021, this term has a subjective definition that ranges from a supernatural entity that is omnipresent and omnipotent to a statue that has been worshiped via Unstudied introjected projection. The word God causes all kinds of issues as it is not well understood and, in most cases, is written off as spooks and a sky daddy belief. What I believe happens is during this knee-jerk reaction to this idea and the term is Pandora box of ignorance opens its doors and eventually has us who have been acculturated mischaracterizing other people's cultural beliefs and worldview the same as the vague and vague oversimplified God concept, we subscribed to. We see a depiction of Maat and think idol; we see Ishango or Ogun and think west African spookism without understanding that these deities have their concepts and their meanings. They use distinct from the Abrahamic religion's God, who in literary reality ironically takes on many different names with different meanings as well when textual criticism is objectively applied to the language it was allegedly initially written in. But for the sake of the discussion for this aspect and moment in time, I won't go that deep because of the oversimplification that I have witnessed on social media. I will simply point by point deal with Atheism, who can be an atheist in a particular context and who couldn't in another and why.

Ankh, on pg. 2 of his publication, states "the word atheist, which generally describes a person "without God "or one that denies God" (West, 2016). The next paragraph Ankh writes is where he utilizes his agency and clarifies what sets him as a Real Black Atheist apart from the regular generic Atheist when he elaborates "an atheist does not acknowledge the differences between black and white cultures they do not support traditional systems and most of the time they correlate African agency as pseudo, therefore, using the European paradigm an atheist is simply "without a god." (West, 2016) He explains the origin of Atheism and mentions Thales of Greece as the father of Atheism conceding to its ideological European birthplace but at the same time demonstrates what made Thales get the label of Atheist, which he states was ideological opposition to the State-sponsored religion God. "Any opposition to those gods meant opposition to that political system. Opposition to the political system made one an atheist; it's a concept that is entirely different from what we understand as Atheism today but hear me and understand that whenever we learn traditional African social system, we become an Atheist. Thereby, anyone who rejects State-sponsored religion became an enemy of the State and by default label an atheist" (West, 2016)

Kofi launches a massive spear into the dialogue in Spears of the Mossi on pg. 98 when he cited a European view of the African pre colonialism. "Before the introduction of genuine faith and higher standards of cultures by the Arabs, the natives had neither a political organization nor strictly speaking any religion, therefore, an examining the pre-Muhammadan conditions of the negro races to confine ourselves to the description of their crude fetishism their brutal and often cannibal customs their vulgar and repulsive idols in their squalid homes" (Frobenius, 1913:pg 12)

He then backdoors with another spear citing, "how can the untutored Africans comprehend God? Deity is a philosophical concept in which savages or incapable of framing" (Pritchard, 1965: 1)

He then defines the terms heathen and pagan in which he elaborates that they mean "one who worships idols or does not acknowledge the true God a rude barbarous and irreligious person" (KPRT, 2020)

Based on the quotes alone, it must be understood why one would take the position that an African is viewed as an atheist in this context. This isn't Ankh, Shawn P, Kofi, or my words; these are white Europeans looking down on the Africans so tough that they felt as if we weren't competent enough to have high cultural standards or genuine faith without Arab assistance. They felt that because they viewed us as savages, the philosophical concept of deity was unobtainable for us even to frame. This is based solely on their subjective and flawed point of view but is a documented HISTORICAL context, nonetheless. While I disagree with the framing, I cannot deny the spoken words or the people saying the words.

These foreigners believed in "God" and felt these other people (Africans) didn't. These Africans did and felt went in opposition to the colonial State-sponsored religion hence the eventual conversion of the Africans to Abrahamic faiths.

To offer the context as to why the African can only be an atheist through the eyes of the Europeans, you must first study Kimoyo. Your 1st have to go down the animism rabbit hole to end up at vitalism to sum it up in a few words "Fu kiau self-healing power and therapy States moyo according to the ancient schools of Africa means vital power, Moyo is the vitality of life. It is the keyword to kibantu, the Bantu way of life their philosophy kimoyo (vitalism) is their religion and isn't animism" (Piesie, 2021). Understanding this, you must understand their concept of deity isn't the same as Abrahamic religions. To explain the difference in my own words, the African deification process is quite different from Abrahamic religion's there is no founder. Everything from the geographic environment to the natural weather phenomenon was a factor in the development of KIMOYO.

Everything venerated is a natural force of some sort, whether it be rain, the energy of lightning, the sustainability of the sun rays, or a river. The things deified in kimoyo are confirmed because they can be identified in nature and have meaning and purpose. Maat isn't simply a female depiction on a relief. Maat is a label for an idea representing the personification of truth, justice, and the cosmic order. The same goes pretty much for most of the continent regarding belief. While some groups may identify a supreme Creator as "god," this deity usually isn't involved in day-to-day human life, and lesser deities are called upon to communicate for you.

The role of the supreme deity in African cosmogony is created via some type of complex process that involves the lesser deities. "In African cosmological narrative, creation is always portrayed as a complex process whether the universe has evolved from a pre-existing matter of Divine thought. (Piesie, 2021)

An Atheist may argue the mere mention of deity would qualify the Africans concept of "God" as the same as any others. I challenge the atheist to attempt to make this same argument with sociological and sociolinguistic understanding and see if it holds merit.

I here wrap my conclusion up with these excerpts from Asar Imhotep's YouTube presentation Atheism is for white people, which I encourage the reader to review in which he substantiates through multiple examples across the continent that in Africa, God equates to existence which I dare not disagree. "According to the Dagara myth of origin, nature itself is a generic auto being and has no creator" (Tengan, 2019)

"Horton shows how the above-mentioned scholars have used Judeo Christian concepts to interpret African thought and assert that such notion of God (Supreme Being), spirits, souls, spirits of the sold and so on are meaningful only to people who have spent years studying and practicing Judeo Christian religion and who have to wish to have a translated version of African thought in Western Christianity." (Tengan, 2019)

"Dagara religion is all about the Cosmos, the cosmic force, the cosmic energy, Cosmic= Everything that is together. You need to know how to interact with Cosmos, and you do it in the form of deity, the form of God, the form of divinity. You give it personality using one of the forces" (from an interview of Alexis Tengan 18:40)

"Maat was the essence of existence which was not only the essence of the creator and humans but also of the natural world" (Karenga, 2006: 198)

"African philosophy is consistent with the philosophical position that motion is the principle of being. According to this understanding, the condition of being with regard to every entity means that to be is to be in the condition of ness. Whatever is perceived as a whole is always a wholeness in the sense that it exists and purses towards that which ii is yet to be. Because this is the character of every existing entity being is to be always understood as the wholeness." (Coetzee and Roux, 2003: 380)

Sources

Meerloo, J. A. M. (1956). The rape of the mind: The psychology of thought control, menticide, and brainwashing. The World Publishing Company. https://doi.org/10.1037/13187-000

Thiessen, E.J. Indoctrination and religious education. Interchange 15, 27–43 (1984). https://doi.org/10.1007/BF01807940

Funk and Wagnalls: "To instruct in doctrines; esp., to teach partisan or sectarian dogmas"; I.A. Snook, ed. 1972. Concepts of Indoctrination (London: Routledge and Kegan Paul).

Little, W. (n.d.) Introduction to sociology - 1st Canadian edition. B.C. Open Textbook project.q https://opentextbc.ca/introductiontosociology/front-matter/about-the-book/

Branch, André J. "Deculturalization". SAGE knowledge. SAGE Publications, Inc. Retrieved 9 November 2014.

Jones, Charles Colcock, 1804-1863 "The Religious Instruction of the Negroes." In the United States:

Electronic Edition.

Anti-Epistemology

2nd November 2014,written by Adriano Mannino

http://crucialconsiderations.org/rationality/anti-epistemology/

Cognitive Dissonance

By Saul McLeod, updated Feb 05, 2018

https://www.simplypsychology.org/cognitive-dissonance.html

DiPaolo, J., Simpson, R.M. Indoctrination anxiety and the etiology of belief. Synthese 193, 3079–3098 (2016). https://doi.org/10.1007/s11229-015-0919-6

(Psychology, n.d)

https://psychology.iresearchnet.com/social-psychology/social-cognition/belief-perseverance/

(Effectiviology, n.d)

https://effectiviology.com/backfire-effect-facts-dont-change-minds/

(Casad, n.d)

https://www.britannica.com/science/confirmation-bias

Pepper, David (1993). Eco-socialism: From Deep Ecology to Social Justice. Routledge. pp. 143–144. ISBN 978-

William Grassie, 2012 "The Sciences of Sacred Scriptures"

https://m.huffpost.com/us/entry/us_1244745

(Bible and theology, n.d)

https://www.bibleandtheology.net/highlights-from-the-history-of-biblical-interpretation-introduction-to-allegorical-interpretation-with-philo/

Audi, Robert (1999). The Cambridge Dictionary of Philosophy (2nd ed.). Cambridge: Cambridge University Press. pp. 377. ISBN 978-0521637220

Zimmermann, Jens (2015). Hermeneutics: A Very Short Introduction. Oxford University Press. p. 2. ISBN 9780199685356.

hermeneutics | Definition & Facts". Encyclopedia Britannica

(Belief, 2003)

https://plato.stanford.edu/entries/belief/

https://dictionary.apa.org/mnemonics

Contemporary Zoroastrians: An Unstructured Nation. Lanham, MD: University Press of America. Zaehner, R.C. 1961. (Zaehner, 20-21)

"The Limits of Faith: The Failure of Faith-based Religions" by Muata Ashby.

: https://a.co/iJOWoDR

(Gunkel 1997, p. lxviii)

(Mazar, Amihay Archaeology of the land of the Bible, 10,000-586 BCE. Garden City, NY: Doubleday. ISBN 978-0385425902. 1992)

 Bright, A History of Israel, 4th ed. (Louisville: Westminster John Knox, 2000), p. 93. 2. William G. Dever, What Did the Biblical Writers Know, and When Did They Know It? What Archaeology Can Tell Us about the Reality of Ancient Israel (Grand Rapids: Eerdmans, 2001), p. 98.

Megan Bishop Moore; Brad E. Kelle (2011). Biblical History and Israel S Past: The Changing Study of the Bible and History. Wm. B. Eerdmans Publishing. p. 62. ISBN 978-0-8028-6260-0.

Dever, William (March 1993). "What Remains of the House that Albright Built?". The Biblical Archaeologist. 56 (1): 25–35. doi:10.2307/3210358. JSTOR 3210358.

Mazar, Amihai (2010). "Archaeology and the Biblical Narrative: The Case of the United Monarchy" (PDF). In Kratz, Reinhard G.; Spieckermann, Hermann; Corzilius, Björn; Pilger, Tanja (eds.). One God – one cult – one nation archaeological and biblical perspectives (Submitted manuscript). Berlin; New York: Walter de Gruyter. pp. 29–58. doi:10.1515/9783110223583.29. ISBN 978-3110223583.

Israel Finkelstein; Neil Asher Silberman (2001). The Bible Unearthed: Archaeology's New Vision of Ancient Israel and the Origin of Sacred Texts. Simon and Schuster. pp. 81–82. ISBN 978-0743223386.

Holland, Thomas A. (1997). "Jericho". In Eric M. Meyers (ed.). The Oxford Encyclopedia of Archaeology in the Near East. Oxford University Press. pp. 220–224.

Kenyon, Kathleen M. (1957). Digging up Jericho: The Results of the Jericho Excavations, 1952–1956. New York: Praeger. p. 229.

Bienkowski, Piotr (1986). Jericho in the Late Bronze Age. Warminster. pp. 120–125.

Finkelstein & Silberman 2001j

Peake's commentary on the Bible

Hatzor – The Head of all those Kingdoms". Retrieved 2018-09-18

Tubb 1998, pp. 13–14

McNutt 1999, p. 47

K. L. Noll, Canaan and Israel in Antiquity: An Introduction, A&C Black, 2001 p. 164:'It would seems that in the eyes of Merneptah's artisans, Israel was a Canaanite group indistinguishable from all other Canaanite groups.' 'It is likely that Merneptah's Israel was a group of Canaanites located in the Jezreel Valley.'

Redford, Donald B. (1992). Egypt, Canaan, and Israel in ancient times. Princeton, NJ: Princeton University Press. p. 305. ISBN 978-0691000862

Spong, John Shelby (1992) Rescuing the Bible from Fundamentalism (Harper)

Finkelstein, Mazar & Schmidt 2007

https://en.m.wikipedia.org/wiki/Historicity_of_the_Bible#CITEREFMazar1992

https://study.com/academy/lesson/the-bible-as-a-historical-document.html

Amesbury 2005

(From the 1907 book by Lyman E. Stowe

Stowe's Bible Astrology: The Bible Founded on Astrology (Kessinger Publishing), pp. 130-136)

The Story of Jesus is an Astrological Allegory for the Sun passing through the Zodiac each year https://www.solarmythology.com/bibleastrology.htm

Pardee, Dennis (1999). "Eloah". In Van der Toorn, Karel; Becking, Bob; Van der Horst, Pieter W. (eds.). Dictionary of Deities and Demons in the Bible (2nd ed.). Leiden: Brill Publishers. p. 285. doi:10.1163/2589-7802_DDDO_DDDO_Eloah. ISBN 90-04-11119-0. The term expressing the simple notion of 'gods' in these texts is ilm...

Van der Toorn 1999, pp. 352–353, 360–364

(Etymonline, n.d) "God" retrieved from

(https://www.etymonline.com/

(Blue letter bible, n.d) " Genesis 1"

Retrieved from https://www.blueletterbible.org/

Doverspike, William F. "How cognitive distortions affect religious fundamentalists." (2016)

Aackerman, C y(n.d)

https://positivepsychology.com/team/courtney-ackerman/

The science of religious beliefs Justin L.BarrettJonathan A.Lanman

Centre for Anthropology and Mind, Oxford University, 58A Banbury Road, Oxford, OX2 6QS retrieved from

https://doi.org/10.1016/j.religion.2008.01.007

Weinberger, A.B., Gallagher, N.M., Warren, Z.J. et al. Implicit pattern learning predicts individual differences in belief in God in the United States and Afghanistan. Nat Commun 11, 4503 (2020). https://doi.org/10.1038/s41467-020-18362

https://www.nature.com/articles/s41467-020-18362-3

"The Scientific Method In Kemet - Sesh Medew Netcher - The Ancient Egyptian Hieroglyphic Writing System" https://seshmedewnetcher.com/the-scientific-method-in-kemet/

Intertextuality (n.d)

https://literaryterms.net/intertextuality/

Tylén.K, Fusaroli.R, Rojo.S, Heimann.K, Fay.N, Johannsen.N.N, Riede,F and Lombard.M

The evolution of early symbolic behavior in Homo sapiens PNAS March 3, 2020 117 (9) 4578-4584; first published February 18, 2020; https://doi.org/10.1073/pnas.1910880117

https://www.pnas.org/content/117/9/4578

Radford. B (2010)

Belief in Witchcraft Widespread in Africa Retrieved from

https://www.livescience.com/amp/8515-belief-witchcraft-widespread-africa.html

"Mangbetu ." Encyclopedia of World Cultures. . Retrieved September 22, 2021 from Encyclopedia.com: https://www.encyclopedia.com/humanities/encyclopedias-almanacs-transcripts-and-maps/mangbetu

University of Iowa Stanley Museum of Art (n.d) ART & LIFE IN AFRICA: Mangbetu https://africa.uima.uiowa.edu/peoples/show/Mangbetu#:~:text=The%20Mangbetu%20creator%20god%20is,that%20their%20ancestors%20be%20venerated.

Marcus. D, "Trans-Substantivity and the Processes of American

Law" (2013) BYU L. Rev. 1191 (2014).

Available at: https://digitalcommons.law.byu.edu/lawreview/vol2013/iss5/4.

Evans, E. M., & Poling, D. (2004). Religious Belief, Scientific Expertise, and Folk Ecology, Journal of Cognition and Culture, 4(3-4), 485-524. doi: https://doi.org/10.1163/1568537042484931

Dimitrios Kapogiannis, Aron K. Barbey, Michael Su, Giovanna Zamboni, Frank Krueger, and Jordan Grafman

PNAS March 24, 2009 106 (12) 4876-4881; https://doi.org/10.1073/pnas.0811717106

https://www.pnas.org/content/106/12/4876.short

Winslow. M, Staver. J , Scharmann.L (2011)

Evolution and personal religious belief: Christian university biology-related majors' search for reconciliation Retrieved from

https://doi.org/10.1002/tea.20417

https://onlinelibrary.wiley.com/doi/abs/10.1002/tea.20417

Price. R (2021)

5 Cognitive Distortions, 5 Biblical Antidotes

Retrieved from https://tacomachristiancounseling.com/articles/5-cognitive-distortions-5-biblical-antidotes

Eremsoy, C., & Inozu, M. (2016). The Role of Magical Thinking, Religiosity and Thought-Control Strategies in Obsessive-Compulsive Symptoms in a Turkish Adult Sample. Behaviour Change, 33(1), 1-14. doi:10.1017/bec.2015.16

Kumar. M (2018)

The Relationship Between Beliefs, Values, Attitudes and Behaviours

Retrieved from"

https://owlcation.com/social-sciences/Teaching-and-Assessing-Attitudes

Merriam-Webster Online Dictionary (2021)

Anti Retrieved from

https://www.merriam webster.com/dictionary/anti#:~:text=or%20someone)%20%3A%20against-,anti%2D,%3A%20against%20someone%20or%20something)

Kofi Piesie Research Team (2020)

Spears of the Mossi: A Historical Survey of the Minds of African Warrior Scholars vol.1

Kofi Piesie (2021)

Beautiful Lessons About Kimoyo

Same Tree Different Branch publishing

Ankh West (2016)

The Chronology of Human Evolution: Real Black Atheism Explained

Conifer, Steven J. (June 2002). "Theological Noncognitivism Examined". The Interlocutor. 4. Archived from the original on January 23, 2004. Retrieved 24 May 2007.

Spiegel, Irving (1965). "Jewish 'Ignostic' Stirs Convention; Dropping of 'God' in Service Deplored and Condoned". New York Times. p. 62.

Frobenius, L. Blind,R. The voice of Africa: Being an account of the travels of the years 1910-1912. Hutchinson & amp Co. 1913

Parkin, D. (1966). E. E. Evans-Pritchard: The position of women in primitive societies, and other essays in social anthropology. 260 pp., 4 plates. London: Faber and Faber Ltd.,1965. 35s. Bulletin of the School of Oriental and African Studies, 29(1), 193-193.

Alexis Bekyane Tengan (2019). Of LIfe and Health. The launguage of ARt and Religion in an African Medical System. New York, Oxford, Berghan.

Interview Alexis Tengan PhD

(Anthropologist: Dagara), YouTube upload by Asar Imhotep June 11, 2020

(from interview of Alexis Tengan 18:40)

https://youtu.be/takBFdHc9IA

Karenga.M (2006: 198)

Maat: The Moral Ideal in Ancient Egypt

The University of Sankore Press

(Coetzee and Roux, 2003: 380) "The African Philosophy Reader" Oxford University Press of Southern Africa

Imhotep, A (2020) "Aaluja: Cyena-Ntu Religion and Philosophy, Vol. II," Philadelphia, Madu Ndela Press

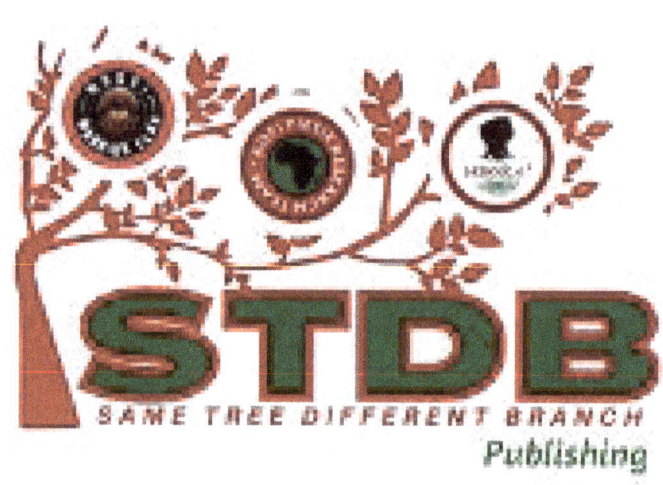

Same Tree Different Branch Publishing 2021 Releases

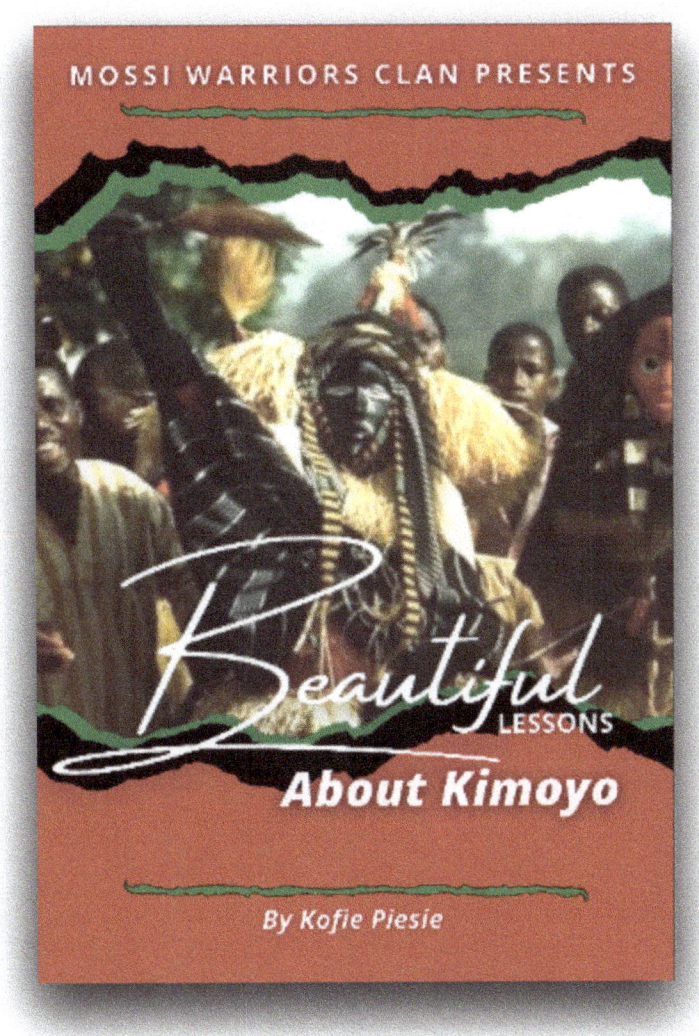

MOSSI WARRIOR CLAN PRESENT

What Sars-CoV₂ Taught Me

By: Ini-Herit Shawn P

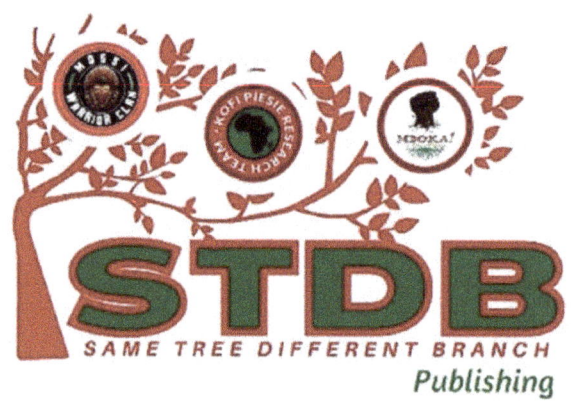

www.ingramcontent.com/pod-product-compliance
Lightning Source LLC
Chambersburg PA
CBHW040315170426
43196CB00020B/2926